Guide to
Interactive Read-Alouds

4-5

Linda Hoyt

Heinemann, Portsmouth, NH

*first*hand
An imprint of Heinemann
361 Hanover Street
Portsmouth, NH 03801-3912
www.firsthand.heinemann.com
www.interactivereadalouds.com

Offices and agents throughout the world

© 2007 by Linda Hoyt

Library of Congress Cataloguing-in-Publications Data
CIP data is on file with the Library of Congress

ISBN-13: 978-0-325-01098-4 (Set)
ISBN-10: 0-325-01098-6

ISBN-13: 978-0-325-01110-3 (Lesson Book)
ISBN 10: 0-325-01110-9

ISBN-13: 978-0-325-01111-0 (Teachers Guide)
ISBN 10: 0-325-01111-7

To learn more about the Interactive Read-Alouds series go to www.interactivereadalouds.com

Printed in the United States of America on acid-free paper

11 10 09 08 07   ML   1 2 3 4 5 6

CONTENTS

Today's read-aloud is a vibrant, deliberate part of good teaching,
an essential, effective strategy for introducing sophisticated
ideas to young learners . . .

—LESTER LAMINACK AND REBA M. WADSWORTH
LEARNING UNDER THE INFLUENCE OF LANGUAGE AND LITERATURE,
FIRST EDITION, BACK COVER

INTERACTIVE READ-ALOUDS

A Vitally Important Tradition

Read-aloud time is much-treasured in most elementary classrooms. This is a time when teachers open windows into the world of mystery, magic, and enormous possibility that resides within the covers of our favorite books. It is a time when we can focus on the most joyous side of reading, helping students to find passion and wonder in the world of print. Read-alouds bind the entire class together, enfolding teacher and students in a shared history of beloved stories and authors.

I love nothing better than seeing wide eyes and bodies leaning forward as I read to fourth and fifth graders. It is amazing how they tell us with their whole physical self when they are engaged in a story and when their imagination and sense of possibility are fully engaged.

In fourth and fifth grades, curriculum demands increase, and there may be a temptation to set aside read-alouds to allow more time for content area instruction and other priorities. I would argue that while content is, of course, important, we must preserve and protect read- aloud time for intermediate age students. We know they still need exposure to rich language and varied text structures. We know they need to fine-tune their ability to reflect upon and consider the craft of writing. We know they need scaffolded support to reach higher levels of interpretive and evaluative thinking. We also know that too few of our students have opportunities to visit museums to see great works of art. Read-alouds based upon Caldecott winners and carefully chosen picture books bring the best of literature and art together in a rich and enticing package, offering us the fullest possible context in which to lift learners to higher levels of understanding.

Read-alouds with award-winning picture books can bring students all of this and more if we:

- select books that link to content area and genre studies in science, social studies, and language arts.
- expect our students to participate fully as thinkers, as language users, and as critical analysts of written language.
- match the standards we strive to teach to beautiful mentor texts so students can see standards in action.

Thoughts from a Pilot Teacher

Sherry Robertson, Grade 5, Walnut Valley, California

I wholeheartedly believe in using picture books to teach reading to upper-grade students. There is a huge misconception that picture books are too "babyish" for the upper elementary student. That way of thinking limits teachers and prevents them from using a very valuable resource. I use vocabulary-rich picture books with a message to teach deeply structured, schema-based comprehension lessons and to create links to other areas of the curriculum. My kids are so engaged when using quality picture books that I recommend picture books to every educator, even high school teachers!

- focus on short texts and picture books to make elements of language, structure, and literary device transparent in a short time span.
- choose books with great intentionality, focusing on the best possible examples of language and art.
- create a culture in which students expect to interact with stories multiple times so they can first digest a story and then revisit it to look deeply into the internal elements that create a great piece of literature or a fine piece of writing.
- integrate think-alouds focused on the richness of a setting, the precision of verb choices, or the humor in an allusion.

When these elements are in place and learners understand that stories have an important role that extends beyond entertainment, we enter the rigorous world of the interactive read-aloud.

English Language Learners: Reading Picture Books

Students who are learning English as an additional language experience particular benefits from picture books. The pagination of picture books naturally breaks the story line into meaningful chunks that are supported by rich illustrations or photographs. When the teacher pauses to turn the page, the student has a moment to process meaning. The illustrations and pauses in the story line are important supports to comprehension for language learners.

Interactive read-alouds increase learner engagement.

In a traditional read-aloud, the teacher reads and occasionally pauses for a discussion in which students raise their hands, sharing one idea at a time. The few who are called upon get to speak while others listen. Sadly, this minimal level of engagement causes many students to disengage and become passive.

During an interactive read-aloud, the conversation patterns are recast. Students come to the meeting area with a conversation partner. They understand that it is their responsibility to *think together* with that partner and replicate or extend the teacher's thinking during the read-aloud. The teacher opens by reading a short passage and then thinks out loud, demonstrating the target standard or strategy. Students begin as active observers, listening carefully because they know they will soon be expected to engage in the same high-quality thinking with a partner. As the read-aloud continues, students are

English Language Learners: Turning & Talking

The Turn & Talk interaction embedded in each *Interactive Read-Alouds* lesson is perfect for English language learners, who typically feel safer with a partner or in a small group setting. You might pair two students with the same primary language so the more competent English speaker can translate and interpret for his or her partner. But even a sensitive English speaker can guide a student who's learning English, simply by paying close attention to the Thinking Partner's needs and intervening as needed. The very nature of the interactive read-aloud makes it a highly supportive instructional context for English language learners.

During Turn & Talk moments, the expectation is for accountable, high-level conversation on the topic. Partner talk is limited to a short burst of 20–30 seconds so students stay focused and don't have time to stray off topic (Jensen, 1998). Careful timing of Turn & Talk moments— approximately once in every five minutes of read-aloud time— ensures that for all students, the learning is full of meaningful talk and that the students have immediate opportunities to use the content vocabulary of the story. This is especially important with informational selections because the partner conversations ensure that students immediately engage as "users" of the vocabulary that is central to the content.

challenged to . . . Turn & Talk! Their task is to think together with their partner about the focus standard or strategy and how it is brought forward in the read-aloud selection. The teacher moves into the group and listens to partners as they share their thinking. After a brief, 20- to 30-second conversation, students are brought back together and the reading continues. Students do not raise their hands until the end of story, when everyone is expected to participate in thinking and reflecting. This creates a setting in which all students are actively involved in thinking, applying strategies, and using language. Everyone is responsible. Everyone is involved. This is learning that is active, energized, and empowering to intermediate age students.

Thoughts from Pilot Teachers

Sally Wells, Grade 4, Beaverton, Oregon

> We enjoyed the Turn & Talk and thinking together. The students like it so much, they remind me to add it to lessons in other portions of the day!

Ann Marie Pawlitsz, Grade 5, North Aurora, Illinois

> The questions and the stopping points for Turn & Talk moments really had the students analyzing the stories. In fact, many of them got into deeper discussions and started asking more questions of me.

Thinking Partners

I am often asked about how Thinking Partners are chosen. I find that with some groups of learners, I can ask them to find a Thinking Partner on their way to our story time area and it works beautifully. They sit with their partner and expect to have responsible conversations together. With some classes, I need to provide extra behavioral support by preselecting Thinking Partners for students. In this case, I want to ensure that I do not match my highest- and lowest-achieving students because the higher achiever may have a tendency to take over and do all of the thinking. This is a good time to be sensitive to the needs of ELL students who may need first-language support and consider matching them with another student who speaks their native language.

In all cases, it is necessary to model Thinking Partner conversations. It is important that students understand that I place high value on quality talk and on taking responsibility for thinking together. To help them understand, I often ask another teacher or a student in class to be my Thinking Partner. We sit facing each other while the students "fishbowl" around us to

listen to our conversation and to notice the way we look directly at our partner, practice active listening, and are careful to take turns talking. As they catch on, then I bring two students to the center of the "fishbowl" to model quality Thinking Partner interactions.

It helps a lot to have a partner pair sit in the center and have the rest of the class circle around and listen to them talk to each other. Notice the way they maintain eye contact, face each other, and listen. Notice the way they share their thinking and try to connect to each other's ideas. Point out, for example, the way Partner B listens carefully and then makes a statement that directly connects to Partner A's thinking. Modeling quality talk and respect for one another will lift Thinking Partners to higher levels of interaction and support learning of the target standards.

Be sure to help the students understand that even though we call this a Turn & Talk, they need to focus on *active listening* with their Thinking Partner. Their time together should include careful listening and then "linking up," in which they extend and elaborate on statements made by their partner. We should hear partners use language such as "I can piggyback on that," "I had a similar idea," and "I wondered about that, too." Their conversations should be connected, focused, and deep.

Once the Turn & Talk reflection is complete, you can return to the read-aloud or—occasionally—celebrate students' thinking by asking partners to share their discoveries and wonderings out loud so others can hear the collaborative reflections.

Through interactive read-alouds, our students can:

- learn to take an active role during the read-aloud experience, sharing their thinking with partners and taking time to talk about their understandings.
- become better listeners as they "Turn & Talk . . . and listen" to their partners.
- learn the power of interactive thinking.
- strengthen comprehension strategies in a setting where they are free to think deeply without being encumbered by decoding.
- make links to social studies and science content.
- establish clear understandings of fluency as they listen to the teacher model phrased, fluid, expressive reading.
- glean ideas and strategies for crafting their own writing.
- explore a variety of genre and appreciate the many shapes and forms written language can assume.
- develop an understanding of literary elements and devices.
- expand vocabulary and literary language while talking about the full range of genre in their lives.

Thoughts from Pilot Teachers

Setrina Byrd and Lauren Schexnider, Wingate, North Carolina

> The lessons are wonderful, and they provoke much deep thinking from the students.

Why aren't novels the focus of these lessons?

We all cherish the time we spend savoring the richly woven tapestry of character development, settings, events, and so on in our favorite novels. However, when our purpose is to teach comprehension strategies, state standards, literary devices, and writing traits, short texts have many advantages. The shorter story lines of picture books make it possible to illuminate a standard and provide guided practice in a relatively short time. This is important as the curriculum load is enormous and there is much to cover. By presenting comprehension strategies and standards in short texts that make the point succinctly, I can quickly support students in considering how to generalize the strategy to other picture books, science texts, historical fiction, and so on. With a well-chosen picture book, strategy lessons are brief and explicit, laying the foundation for application of the learning in content area resources as well as in additional stories and novels.

Visible Record of Learning

As *Interactive Read-Alouds* lessons are presented over time, I keep a record of our picture-book explorations. (See the "Record of Interactive Read-Alouds" on pages 51–53.) I record the standards that we explore together and the mentor texts we use to explore these important understandings. Then, as we read content area selections, news magazines, short stories, and novels, students can refer to the chart of literary devices already studied and make connections to both the device and the mentor texts. I often see students searching for an original picture book mentor text to make a point to a partner as they are discussing a novel! The foundation laid by the interactive read-aloud with a short text enables learners to see the rich interweaving of text elements in a novel and empowers them to think more deeply. Interactive read-alouds are a springboard, helping students to take more responsibility for their learning when they connect with a story, extend a strategy, or make links between fiction and nonfiction selections.

Thoughts from a Pilot Teacher

Jill Wilson, Grade 5, Walnut Valley, California

> I have loved the picture book lessons. My fifth graders have really enjoyed the shorter yet in-depth stories. I feel like I am teaching them such different things than before. We are loving the lessons, and comprehension is going up a ton! Thank you for letting me participate in the pilot testing of these lessons!

Multiple Read-Alouds a Day

Whenever possible, I advocate for multiple read-alouds each day—one fiction, one nonfiction, and one for the "art" of it. While this may sound like another challenge to our overloaded days with learners, it can actually fit in quite nicely. Knowing that you are likely to have a novel as an ongoing read-aloud, you might consider shortening your novel read-aloud by a few minutes each day. This would make room for a mentor text read-aloud experience in either fiction or nonfiction that would be interactive and set the stage for deeper thinking in the novel and in content area studies. Because the mentor books are short texts, they can be read fairly quickly and nestled more easily into the learning day.

I believe it is essential to ensure that read-alouds occur in both fiction and nonfiction. We *must* expose our students to the language forms and structures of these two highly diverse text forms. The language of a math book, a set of directions, a science resource, and a newspaper all differ dramatically from the language of a novel or a picture book. If our students are to be empowered readers in all the texts of their world and the assessments they must navigate, we must ensure they have ample opportunity to listen to the language of these varied nonfiction formats.

Nonfiction read-alouds can be woven into content area studies such as science, social studies, or health. Please consider the power of having you, not a student, open a science or social studies time with a read-aloud. With you as the model for expressive, fluid, and meaningful reading, students will attend more closely and demonstrate a higher level of engagement. Reading aloud even a paragraph or two sets the stage for attention and deep thinking while showing that your interest in the topic is so significant that *you* are honoring the topic with a brief read-aloud. An expressive teacher read-aloud from a textbook or a science or social studies resource gives the material higher status with learners and increases their investment in the topic.

Nonfiction picture books can make this even more exciting. Seymour Simon, for example, has written more than 100 titles on topics ranging from the solar system to the human body to gorillas. If you keep his books and those of other wonderful nonfiction authors close at hand, you can open a lesson on the solar system with a brief read-aloud from the beginning pages of one of his books, such as *Mars* or *The Sun*. A page or two of his rich, enticing language is a tremendous opener to a learning segment, and I promise you that your students will compete for access to these gorgeous books so they can keep reading!

The read-aloud for the "art" of it takes only a few seconds and is easily woven into transition times such as putting away resources to prepare for another subject. I simply ask the students to be especially quiet during the transition because I am going to share something special with them. This might be a quick poem, a news brief, a short passage from a novel, or the lead to a picture book. I add a layer of dimension to the moment by playing soft instrumental music in the background while reading. This sets the tone, signifies the moment as special, and creates a sense of drama that really captures students' attention. The idea is to use transition moments that might otherwise be wasted and transform them into one more opportunity to share rich and beautiful language with our learners. As students go about their tasks of regrouping for a new topic, there is a hush as the music begins and I present a poem, a paragraph, or a few lines from the lead to a powerful book. I leave the music on when I finish, encouraging students to savor the moment before they begin speaking again.

As fourth and fifth graders catch on to the concept of "reading for the art of it," I have partners sign up to select and prepare the "artistic" reading of the day. This adds responsibility for the students and enables them to participate more fully in their own learning.

Once the multiple read-alouds are in place in my learning day, I then need to select one read-aloud to become the interactive read-aloud for the day. I don't want to interrupt every book with talk or to dissect each piece of literature or poem. We must have a clear and careful balance between reading for the joy of it and reading to deepen our knowledge of how print works and how we construct meaning.

PRINCIPLES AND PRACTICE THAT GUIDE *INTERACTIVE READ-ALOUDS*

The interactive read-aloud lessons in this collection bring together students and classic picture books to promote learning on multiple fronts. Several principles or beliefs about read-aloud practice guided their development.

> Informational texts comprise the vast majority of texts that readers face in middle school, high school, standardized assessments, and the print they will encounter for the rest of their lives. We must take very seriously the importance of teaching them *how* to navigate informational texts.

Powerful "mentor texts"—exemplary children's classics and strong nonfiction texts—are the centerpiece of *Interactive Read-Alouds.*

Students deserve opportunities to interact with the richest language, most beautiful art, and most engaging story lines that we can offer. In selecting mentor texts, books that could serve as exemplary models for readers and writers, we turned to the gorgeous art and enticing story lines of Caldecott winners as well as treasured favorites. These books offer characters and plots that enthrall our learners, texts that you will want to revisit over and over again, and topics that will expand students' knowledge of the world. You will also notice a carefully constructed strand of award-winning biographies plus nonfiction by masters such as Seymour Simon and Walter Wick.

Mentor Texts

The concept of a mentor text is important. A mentor is one who models, coaches, and lifts another to higher levels. With that in mind, a mentor text must be chosen carefully to ensure that it can establish a model of quality writing that is worthy of guiding our

learners. With the help of a beautifully crafted mentor text, we can wonder together about imagery, possible themes, and the elements that have come together to create the literary magic that resides in these much-loved books. Nonfiction mentor books are a wonderful way to accustom students to the kinds of text structures they'll encounter in informational texts.

With a mentor text in hand, we can gently open our students' eyes to the inner workings of a selection, savor its beauty, and create powerful links to the standards we want our students to understand. The mentor texts profiled in these lessons were chosen for characteristics that support all intermediate age learners, native speakers and English language learners alike.

English Language Learners: Using Mentor Texts

The visual nature of picture book read-alouds makes these lessons powerful literacy experiences for English language learners. The illustrations support the language of the story, building rich contexts and encouraging connections to the learners' native language. To ensure comprehension, you may want to have a pre-reading conversation with your ELL students to build academic vocabulary and schema for the story. Adding realia and dramatic interpretations can also enhance the read-aloud experience for children who are learning English as an additional language (Cary, 2000).

Booklinks

The mentor text lessons in *Interactive Read-Alouds* are a beginning, a springboard from which the true learning grows. We know that students' control over strategies gains strength as strategies are transferred across multiple reading experiences. Therefore, the Lesson Matrix on pages 54–57 lists Booklinks—recommended titles that will help you stretch the learning across multiple texts. Booklinks become critical for students as they enter a journey of deep understanding.

After an initial lesson with the mentor text, it is important to turn to the Booklinks and continue expanding the strategy across multiple reading selections. What is important is that the strategy focus be clearly modeled in the mentor text and then extended across multiple subject areas so students can synthesize their learning. With each Booklink lesson, students will develop strength and flexibility with the target learning, culminating in a level of application that is deeper and stronger than a single lesson could ever produce. Booklinks are important scaffolds that develop long-term understanding.

> J ust because you complete the mentor text and lesson doesn't mean it is time to stop working on the standard or strategy.

You will notice that the Booklinks offer a rich mix of familiar favorites, Caldecott winners, and Newbery winners. Each one was carefully chosen as an exemplar for the target learning or an opportunity to stretch the target learning into a different genre. To create your Booklinks lessons, use the Lesson Planner that is provided on pages 37–38 and on the *Printable Resources* CD-ROM.

I choose the interactive experience carefully, and then I plan for long-term learning that will carry from the interactive read-aloud across Booklinks, related stories, nonfiction selections, shared readings, and Readers Theater experiences. With essential standards and literary elements as our target, we need to teach to full and complete understanding so our readers can be flexible and strategic in applying their learning across a wide range of texts.

Thoughts from Pilot Teachers

Marie Govro and Leah Starkovich, Portland, Oregon

We were so pleased to find that the mentor texts and Booklinks are readily available in our media center. We love Caldecott books and the opportunity to showcase them in concert with the standards we need to teach. Students are quickly making links between the mentor texts, their novels, and content area reading.

The Power of Rereading

"We must teach our students that rereading is powerful and that when readers reread, they read *differently*" (Franki Sibberson quoted in Hoyt, 2005, page 130). When you reread

a book, you don't have to wonder how it's going to end or what happens to the characters. You can, instead, peel back deeper layers of meaning, noticing the role of literary devices and elements of the writer's craft that would have been too difficult to focus on while unfolding a story for the first time. Rereading can allow us to uncover layers of meaning gradually and with increasing sensitivity to the content and style of the selection.

With this in mind, there was a deliberate effort to utilize mentor selections for more than one standard or strategy. It was also a conscious choice to ensure that titles appear as Booklinks for multiple standards. I often tell students that we are going to reread a selection "with new eyes," to help us to focus deeply on setting, imagery, tension, or the author's voice. Each time we reread with a new purpose, the author's craft becomes more transparent, and students notice more of the inner workings that make imagery, metaphor, or personification so powerful. It is important to celebrate these books again and again and again, each time peeling away another layer of craft to help students realize how richly woven and intricate quality writing can be.

Nonfiction

The lessons in *Interactive Read-Alouds* were built around mentor texts that are the easiest for you to find in schools, public libraries, and bookstores. These books are time-tested favorites and award winners that are least likely to go out of print. There is, however, a sad feature to the convenience of selecting books that are readily available. Caldecott books and treasured favorites with easy availability are primarily fiction. While fiction is, of course, wonderful...it isn't enough. Our learners deserve to have the same in-depth experience and knowledge of nonfiction titles that they have with fiction. They deserve to have rich interactions with nonfiction read-alouds that not only capture kid-delightful, eye-popping information but also sing with exquisite language (Bridges, 2006). They deserve to see that nonfiction texts can capture their interest, pique a sense of wonder, and bring the world alive with striking visuals and vivid language.

Because there is not an established body of familiar nonfiction books readily available in all libraries, broadening your students' nonfiction experience with the target standards

Read the books multiple times for multiple purposes. Every time you revisit a familiar and much loved favorite, it is like welcoming a special friend back into your life. If you enrich the experience even further by encouraging students to view the book with new eyes and look for subtle changes in setting, notice well chosen words the author has used, or pay special attention to the way a character changes and develops, you lift students' understanding and help them see more deeply into the craft of the writer.

and comprehension strategies of these lessons will depend on you. I highly encourage you to go to your library and gather books by Seymour Simon, Gail Gibbons, Stephen Kramer, Walter Wick, Michael Tunnell, and the many other amazing writers of nonfiction that will delight and intrigue your students. Then, using these books as additional Booklinks, model for your students how you can apply comprehension strategies and standards, such as main idea or word choice, as you read a variety of selections. This will help your students in myriad ways. They will be learning about the world. They will again realize that these standards and strategies will help them in any book they read. They will feel empowered as readers because they will have meaning-seeking skills that they have practiced so well, they can apply them in all the texts they encounter.

I enthusiastically promote the power of nonfiction read-alouds and have developed several resources to that end, including *Make It Real: Strategies for Success with Informational Texts* (Heinemann, 2002); *Exploring Informational Texts* (Heinemann, 2003); and *Navigating Informational Texts* video collection (Heinemann, 2004). I believe that learners of all ages need to understand the structure and features of informational texts, experience the wonder and excitement of learning something fascinating about our world, and develop a sense of passion for nonfiction that will show in their eyes and voices when you bring out a new nonfiction book to share. I encourage you to gather wonderful magazines, books, and resources that allow you to extend your students' focus on a strategy into nonfiction. Use the Lesson Planner on pages 37–38 and on the *Printable Resources* CD-ROM to structure your own interactive read-aloud lessons using nonfiction selections.

> **A**cademic purpose: Just for fun is good. It has absolute merit. We must be cautious, however, in making sure that our read-alouds are building a stronger, richer base of literary understanding in the lives of our learners. We must be certain that at least some read-alouds will be laying a foundation for academic success. Is there academic value? How will this read-aloud lift these students to a higher level of performance?

Interactive Read-Alouds lessons have a clear instructional focus that lifts student achievement.

Standards that are commonly held across many states are the driving force throughout these lessons. Each lesson, with its accompanying mentor text and Booklinks, is designed to help students see a standard in action within the supportive and safe context of a read-aloud. Teacher think-aloud language and questions to stimulate quality partner conversations are all focused on the target standard so that students can listen to the teacher applying the standard and then share their thinking with a partner. This process is repeated with each mentor text because teacher modeling and guided practice are central support systems across the many books in which students apply the target standards.

Standards-Based Language

You'll notice that in the lessons I use the language of the standards when talking to the students. I believe that students should use the literary terminology and language that characterize our thinking about comprehension, literary elements, genres, and devices. Fourth- and fifth-grade students need to be comfortable talking about hyperbole, onomatopoeia, inference, critical analysis, interpretation, and so on. These terms are central to students' development as readers, writers, and test takers. We all know how commonly these words appear on the contemporary standardized tests that have become a reality for students at this level.

When you model the use of these terms, and students immediately apply them as they converse with Thinking Partners, the literary language becomes part of their personal academic vocabulary. This explicit, content-driven vocabulary enables students to label the cognitive processes they are using and to accurately categorize the elements that build the rich infrastructure that holds a well-crafted text together.

Thoughts from Pilot Teachers

Sally Wells, Grade 4, Beaverton, Oregon

> Through *Interactive Read-Alouds,* students embrace the terminology of inferring, building upon schema, literal questions versus interpretive.... The conversations around the selections they are reading are richer and reflect the terminology used in the read-aloud. They are cultivating a keen awareness of the power picture books have for a reader and the vocabulary we use to describe our understandings.

Marie Govro, Reading Specialist, Portland, Oregon

> I used the *Cheyenne Again* lesson, "Form Literal and Interpretive Questions." The lesson went so well!! I was truly amazed at the higher level of thinking my students were able to achieve. The questions they were proposing made me sit up and take notice. Thank you! It was then a smooth transition into writing. Students were able to support their thinking by finding evidence in the book. You should have seen their published work! Wow!

Standards-Based Strands

The *Interactive Read-Alouds* lessons are grouped into six standards-based strands: comprehension, structural elements, vocabulary/literary language, literary elements and devices, genre, and writing traits. Each of these strands was selected with great care after an extensive review of standards across the country to determine which standards appear as common threads across multiple states.

COMPREHENSION. This strand focuses on strategies that help learners negotiate the meaning of texts. Within this strand, you will find familiar skills, such as identifying main idea, identifying cause and effect, analyzing, inferring, and comparing/contrasting, that commonly appear in lists of standards for comprehension.

STRUCTURAL ELEMENTS. This strand focuses on elements of story structure. This includes identifying events in a plot sequence, discerning tone and mood, tracking character development, developing a statement of theme for a text, and so on. There is also support for examining structural elements such as climax, setting, problem/solution, and dialogue.

VOCABULARY/LITERARY LANGUAGE. Standards in this strand encourage learners to observe the power of precise vocabulary; identify and appreciate onomatopoeia, literary language, simile, and metaphor; and discern the meanings of unfamiliar words through context clues. Transition words are also highlighted in this strand.

LITERARY ELEMENTS AND DEVICES. Literary elements and devices, such as point of view, foreshadowing, symbolism, irony, and poetic justice, get at the heart of the way an author structures a text to effectively tell a story. Standards in this strand involve readers in more complex story structures and more sophisticated language devices, such as allusion and personification.

> Students often make really charming and insightful comments and observations during a read-aloud—fine for a listen-for-pleasure experience—but the *Interactive Read-Alouds* lesson has a clear and focused learning target—the standard. So all comments and conversations need to maintain a focus on this solitary goal. When our teaching and student thinking are converged on a single point of learning, learners are more likely to notice the standard, understand it, and *apply* it. Then, on future experiences with the book, they can reread with new eyes to notice other powerful points in the same selection.

GENRE. Each genre category—fiction, nonfiction, biography, fairy tale, and so on—has a particular kind of content or structure. While exploring the standards in this strand, learners begin to understand the distinguishing features of various genres and learn what to expect from each.

WRITING TRAITS. Engaging, well-written texts provide outstanding models for writers. Standards in this strand explore ideas, organization, voice, conventions, and so on, so learners can begin to emulate a writer's work and incorporate those traits into their own writing. Links between the craft elements of the mentor texts and student writing are clearly stated so students understand how to replicate the work of their mentors.

"Bull's-Eye" Concept

Each of the *Interactive Read-Alouds* lessons represents a "bull's-eye" session and its extensions. During a bull's-eye instructional session, I home in on one particular strategy or idea in a piece of text. Instruction focuses on a *single standard*. This is not to say that this is the only direction a reading might take; a text might be a mentor book for both point of view and transition words, for example. Each book is rich with possibilities for instruction. The trick is to target one standard per session and outline it so clearly that it becomes transparent for the students. To address additional standards, read the book again on another day and focus on a new teaching point.

Teach to the bull's-eye. Select a point and teach it with great intentionality. Don't allow yourself to be distracted by other possible teaching points. The goal is to narrow the students' field of vision so they can truly see a fine point, study it, and prepare to apply their learning in an authentic and meaningful way.

The Gradual Release of Responsibility

Pearson and Gallagher (1983) coined the phrase "gradual release of responsibility" to describe the idea that instruction should begin with explicit modeling by the teacher, continue with guided practice, and move on to activities that position students to become independent learners. The *Interactive Read-Alouds* lessons you find here are built on just such a model.

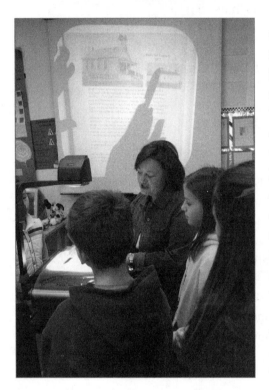

During the Interactive Read-Aloud: Model and Guide Practice segment of each lesson, students see an expert at work. The teacher models think-alouds to provide students with a window into a reading strategy and show how an accomplished thinker uses that strategy. This is especially important for fourth- and fifth-grade students. These students are still learning to read and to navigate ever more complex learning tasks. They need explicit modeling and coaching to see how proficient readers navigate complex ideas and content. Perhaps more than ever, fourth and fifth graders need to see you in action, thinking aloud, modeling, and explaining how you navigate a text. I believe strongly that we should never ask students to do something *they haven't seen their teacher do first*. When we do more modeling, and less assigning, our students get a much stronger sense of what they are to do and make a more concise effort to lift themselves to the expected level of performance.

After modeling and thinking aloud, the teacher provides scaffolds for students as they stretch their new learning into another context. Carefully constructed learning activities in Share the Reading/ Thinking provide guided practice, with the teacher actively support-

Thoughts from a Pilot Teacher

Carol Chiorian, Hudson, Ohio

The lessons allowed me to introduce strategies to the students that will help improve their language arts skills. The read-aloud mentor books were grade-appropriate materials that the students could understand, make connections to, and reread to improve their fluency. Thank you for allowing me to be a part of this process. Your strategies have changed my teaching.

ing the learning in this additional context. During the Readers Theater experience, students get further guided practice as they work with peers. Finally, in Extend the Learning, students attempt the strategy in an independent way.

Infusion of Formal Language

Like the gradual-release model that underpins the *Interactive Read-Alouds* lesson design, the sample test items in each lesson's Infusion of Formal Language feature provide a gentle way to accustom students to the language of tests and, ultimately, to strengthen learners' responsibility for their own performance. The test questions that characterize standardized tests, end-of-unit tests, and so on are written in a formal register that is very different from oral speech and certainly different from most of the literature we read to our students (Hoyt, 2006). Embedding test-style language into your daily interactions with students and weaving this formal register into your conversations about books will help learners to become comfortable with these often unfamiliar structures.

The Infusion of Formal Language section in each lesson gives you sample language to offer your students. The idea is to get them used to hearing these language structures, to think about what the question is really asking of them . . . and then to use these forms to wonder together about the mentor text. The objective isn't just to answer the question correctly. It is to develop a sense of confidence with formal test-style language and to examine the "genre of test."

"Test" as a Genre

Testing is a genre that is totally unique. To help our students understand the features and strategies of navigating test-style questions, we must also help them consider the "genre of test." What are its attributes? What do we know about the structure of a test question? What are the rules when you play the "game of test"? As

students consider the sample questions, encourage them to think like a test writer. If they were going to create a test-style question about the book, what would it sound like? In which position (A, B, C, D) would they place the correct answer? Why are the distractors often designed to trick a reader?

Once familiar with using a formal language register to talk about books, fourth and fifth-grade students love creating their own test-style questions. To support them, I create a poster of "stems" commonly used in test questions. Teams select a stem from which to generate a question about a book; then they begin the challenge of creating the four possible answers. They quickly catch on to the idea of placing the correct answer first and then arranging "distractors" that are almost correct around it. I further extend their understanding of test as a genre with more challenging stems, such as "Which of the following is NOT true?" This challenges them to create three correct responses and only one that is not true. Students love creating charts with their questions and responses and then quizzing each other.

The samples of test-style questions and formal language in each lesson are provided as springboards. You may want to post a list of common test-style stems and then deliberately use them as you talk with students about the books and stories you share. Refer to *Spotlight on Comprehension* (Hoyt, Heinemann, 2005, p. 367) for a more comprehensive list.

Interactive Read-Alouds transform a classroom into a learning community.

Share the Reading/Thinking

One of the best ways to immerse students in rich language and extended learning is through shared reading and shared thinking. In these lessons, overhead transparencies present text in a way that is highly visible to all. During Share the Reading or Share the Thinking, a transparency is placed on the overhead using the master provided in the lesson. The teacher and students read the selection aloud and then think together about the target standard. In this new context, the students will need to stretch their understanding of the standard to apply it in a different situation. This supports the transfer of the learning and increases the likelihood that students will take personal and independent control of the standard that is targeted in the lesson.

Best of all, the students are now *reading*. The shift from listening during the read-aloud to reading a text on the overhead increases students' time with text. This provides additional exposure to print and fosters fluency development as the lesson

---

Sample Test-Style Stems

This story is mostly about _____.

In this passage, we could infer that _____.

A good title for this story would be _____.

The best answer is _____.

Which sentence best tells _____?

All of the above.

None of the above.

Which of the following is not true?

What would most likely happen after the end of the story?

In the selection, _____ means _____.

A synonym for _____ would be _____.

encourages multiple readings of the selection for fluency and expression. In the Tip for Share the Reading, you will find suggestions for modeling the reading, reading in unison, reading in teams that alternate lines of text, and so on. Celebrate these rereadings as opportunities to support fluency as well as apply the standard. Underachieving students, in particular, will ben-

efit from choral reading that helps them to float on the shared voices of their peers.

In some lessons, Share the Reading/Thinking becomes an opportunity for you to model writing for the students. This is a wonderful chance for learners to see a proficient writer craft text while they watch the punctuation, spelling, grammar, and word choice unfold on the overhead projector or a chart. Just as the mentor text is a model for reading, you become a model for the quality writing that your students are expected to generate.

Readers Theater

The Readers Theater scripts that are provided with each lesson bring exciting elements to the read-aloud—expressive oral reading and drama! A Readers Theater script may be a retelling of the read-aloud selection, a standards-based experience with a different genre or topic, or an opportunity to learn more about the content explored by the mentor text. The scripts are designed to give students an authentic purpose for oral reading and are specifically crafted to support the target standard. Best of all, they are terrific vehicles for joyful, expressive oral reading that will build fluency in a way that makes it clear to students that fluency isn't just about *fast*. It is about interpreting a selection and matching your rate, intonation, and phrasing to the meaning and the style of text you are sharing.

The scripts are flexible enough to accommodate emergent and developing readers but include concepts and ideas that are engaging for all readers. The scripts afford students opportunities to read different types of text (including nonfiction and poetry) and to become

more fluent readers. Be sure to notice the Tip for Readers Theater Script in each lesson.

The point of Readers Theater is to make readers the stars! While Readers Theater gives students opportunities for increasing fluency and vocabulary, improving comprehension, and communicating in a meaningful way, it's also a lot of fun!

To ensure that we maximize time with text, be sure to have students work in small groups to practice and rehearse scripts. This way, all students are reading and participating, and everyone does more reading. If you elect to have students perform their scripts, you can have teams perform for each other or have students perform their scripts for students in other classrooms.

Thoughts from Pilot Teachers

Beth Martin and Joan Wimer, Grade 5, Lancaster, Pennsylvania

> Kids love Readers Theater—no matter what! It was nice to have Readers Theater scripts that were a direct connection to the skill/ subject we just focused on in the interactive read-aloud. Fifth graders still benefit from the fluency practice, and their expressiveness as oral readers really improved!

Differentiating Readers Theater Scripts

If you have below-level readers who need support with the Readers Theater scripts, you may want to incorporate some of the following scaffolds:

- Have the students listen to the script before attempting to read it. They can listen to a peer or a parent volunteer. As students perform scripts, I often turn on a tape recorder and save the recording so developing readers can listen to it before attempting to participate in orally reading the same script.

- Engage students in working with partners to read and discuss the script before performing it.

- Assign challenged students the portions of the script with less reading, until the script becomes familiar. Then switch parts and give the lower-achieving students a chance to shine with a really big part!

- Provide a copy of the Share the Reading passage in lieu of the Readers Theater script. Because this passage has been rehearsed in Shared Reading, it should be comfortable reading for even your lower-achieving students.

- Allow students to rehearse and practice multiple times so they never read aloud unless they are shining with the best reading possible.

- Assign partners to read each part of the script. Multiple voices carry one another over the tough spots and support lower achievers in experiencing success.

- Readers Theater can be easily supported by pantomime and dramatic action. Have lower-achieving students dramatize while

others read as a first experience. Then invite them to rehearse and practice the now familiar script until it is their turn to perform as the readers.

- Use Readers Theater scripts from the grade 2/3 version of *Interactive Read-Alouds* to create a multi-level support system for students in your classroom.

Putting Mentor Books into Students' Hands

The mentor books that are the foundation of each lesson are best enjoyed up close. Whenever possible, I obtain multiple copies of the mentor selections and use them in a variety of ways.

INDEPENDENT READING

Slide mentor books into the independent reading collection of below-level students. Because the story line is familiar, a mentor book is more easily read than a selection the student has not yet heard. The familiar text will support and lift their independent reading and provide an additional invitation to explore the standard associated with the mentor text.

LITERATURE DISCUSSION GROUPS

Sometimes I have small groups meeting all around the room, each with a different mentor book. I then have the teams examine their mentor books for voice, personification, simile, or some other trait we are trying to support. They reread to look for that element and conduct a discussion about the way their author utilized that trait. Then teams share and compare their observations with other teams. This usually leads to wonderful experiences with team writing, where students share the pen to create a piece of writing that exemplifies the craft element or trait they are considering. Making mentor books the focus of a literature discussion group is sure to capture attention, stimulate additional reading, and build confidence with print.

SMALL GROUP INSTRUCTION

Making the read-aloud texts available for small group instruction is another way to increase time with text and lift learner achievement. Once students have had the opportunity to listen to a story and discuss it with a Thinking Partner, they will want to revisit these favorite texts again and again.

This is particularly helpful for ELL students or students who are reading below level. An in-depth reading

experience with the familiar mentor text allows them to reach higher as readers; they already understand the story line, so they can read to fine-tune their interaction with the page and receive direct coaching in strategy use. During small group moments, it is vital to assess students' understanding and reteach as necessary.

WRITING GROUPS

Gather small, guided writing groups to examine elements of the writer's craft in a mentor text. In this case, I would have students reread to think like a writer, locating elements of craft that they can replicate in their own writing.

Creating Space for Interactive Read-Alouds

Interactive read-alouds are intensely social learning experiences. They require a space to gather as a group. Students must be close enough to clearly see the illustrations as these are so important in picture books. They also need immediate proximity to their Thinking Partners as they Turn & Talk. The objective is to bring learners closely together in a learning community. Proximity increases attention to both the teacher and the content being presented. Sitting on the floor, in particular, encourages partner interaction, physical response to learning, and higher levels of engagement (Hoyt, 2003; Harvey, 2001; Routman, 2003; Wolfe, 2001; Jensen, 1998).

Sitting on the floor may have particular benefits because the physical action of moving from point A to point B reignites attention and supports cognitive retention of content. Reinforcing new material kinesthetically has an enormously powerful effect. Even shifting from looking at the teacher to looking at a partner or standing to read a passage can positively affect learning. One elementary school in North Carolina, having implemented Turn & Talk plus kinesthetic interactions, found its state-mandated test results reaching such highs that the state actually sent in officials to ensure that the school was not cheating!

We have a responsibility to create learning environments that engage movement, a sense of learning community, and proximity to the task. Learners seated at desks many feet away from the teacher and the target learning are less likely to pay attention and tend to remember less.

When students remain at their seats without close proximity to the mentor text, they often miss out on important visual clues in the illustrations and lack the sense of community that is created when everyone is together. It is essential, therefore, to look closely at the environment you create for interactive read-alouds and be sure there is a community gathering area where students can gather close to you, share their thinking, and move their bodies!

The very essence of an interactive experience requires that students, teacher, and the mentor text all be in close proximity to heighten visibility, build interest, and craft deep conversations that lift learning. Interactive read-alouds nurture a community of learners who think together, learn together, and grow together.

FITTING *INTERACTIVE READ-ALOUDS* INTO THE CURRICULUM

The *Interactive Read-Alouds* lessons are based on critical standards and comprehension strategies that are essential supports to reader development. The content is indispensable and is firmly rooted in established standards and strategies. While the content is grounded in core

understandings, the lessons themselves are designed to be flexible and merge with your existing curriculum. Your path through the lessons might be governed by a variety of factors:

- You might look at the scope and sequence of an adopted program and then select *Interactive Read-Alouds* lessons to match the program goals and timelines. This would offer strong cross-curricular links for students, connect read-alouds to the core program, and present extended experiences with strategies and standards to ensure transferability of the learning.

- As you engage in curriculum mapping using your state's or district's standards, you could write *Interactive Read-Alouds* lessons right into your plans to coordinate with the standards you plan to address.

- You could use the Lesson Matrix on pages 54–57 as a standards-based planning tool, knowing that the majority of your standards for comprehension, literary elements, and analytical traits can be easily found and supported by the lessons. With this as a base, you could then link your small group instruction and other supports to match the standards emphasis begun during read-aloud.

- You might partner the *Interactive Read-Alouds* mentor texts to novels that exhibit the same literary devices and standards and guide the students in making connections between the craft and style of the two authors.

- You might look for opportunities to tie mentor text lessons to themes in your curriculum. For example, if your students are learning about discrimination, you could cluster *My Brother Martin* by Christine King Farris, *The Other Side* by Jacqueline Woodson, *Pink and Say* and *The Butterfly* by Patricia Polacco, *Drummer Boy* by Ann Turner, and *Under the Quilt of Night* by Deborah Hopkinson. If your topic is westward migration, you might cluster *Dakota Dugout* by Ann Turner and *Cheyenne Again* and *Dandelions* by Eve Bunting. Clustering picture books and novels by theme gives learners an opportunity to apply content vocabulary across multiple texts while still exploring the variety of standards presented in the *Interactive Read-Alouds* lessons.

- The Lesson Matrix (pages 54–57) is a tremendously helpful tool that will support you in moving in and out of the lessons. With the matrix in hand, you may choose to focus on a strand of standards, looking deeply into dimensions of comprehension, writing, or literary analysis. The matrix may help you to pick and choose pieces that fit other curricular initiatives or topic studies. It will also help you to quickly and effectively differentiate because you can so easily match lessons to observable needs in your students.

Choosing a Lesson by Standard

The Lesson Matrix (see pages 54–57) is organized by strand and by standard and matches the order of the lessons. There is at least one lesson (two for Writing Traits) for each standard. The Lesson Matrix shows you the page on which the lesson can be found, the instructional (standard) focus of the lesson, and the title of the mentor text the lesson uses. Booklinks suggest other titles that lend themselves to teaching the target standard.

LESSON MATRIX

Standards for COMPREHENSION

Page Ref	Standard	4/5 Mentor Text	Booklink 1	Booklink 2	Booklink 3	Booklink 4	Booklink 5
1	Activate and apply prior knowledge	*Two Bad Ants*	More Than Anything Else	Wall, The	Martin's Big Words	Yellow Star, The	Number the Stars
7	Form literal and interpretive questions	*Cheyenne Again*	Faithful Elephants	Passage to Freedom	Mysteries of Harris Burdick, The	Wilma Unlimited	Sign of the Beaver
13	Make connections	*Dandelions*	Ox-Cart Man	Thank You, Mr. Falker	Dakota Dugout	Train to Somewhere, The	Stone Fox
19	Connect to the culture/ experiences of others	*Annie and the Old One*	So Far from the Sea	Black Whiteness	Knots on a Counting Rope	All the Places to Love	Bud, Not Buddy
25	Analyze critically	*Yellow Star, The*	Table Where Rich People Sit, The	So You Want to Be President?	Faithful Elephants	Man Who Walked Between the Towers, The	Number the Stars
31	Interpret	Harris	Sno...			G...	The

Choosing a Lesson by Book Title

The Title List (see pages 58–72) contains all the mentor texts and Booklinks listed alphabetically by title. It notes the standard(s) each mentor text is used to teach and identifies standards for which the title makes a good Booklink. Use the Title List to locate a standards-based lesson for a book you have on hand or as a guide to stocking your school or classroom library.

The lessons and books suggested here are, of course, only a fraction of what is possible in your classroom. Any carefully chosen text can become the foundation for an effective interactive read-aloud lesson. The "Lesson Planner for an Interactive Read-Aloud" section (see page 34 and the *Printable Resources* CD-ROM) contains suggestions for choosing texts and a lesson template to guide your lesson planning.

TITLE LIST

Book Title, Author, and Publisher	Mentor Lessons Strand/Standard	Booklinks Strand/Standard
Alexander and the Terrible, Horrible, No Good, Very Bad Day Judith Viorst Atheneum	Vocabulary/Literary Language/Repetition Comprehension/Determine purpose	
All the Places to Love Patricia MacLachlan Joanna Cotler	Writing Traits/Sentence fluency	Comprehension/Connect to the culture/ experiences of others Vocabulary/Literary Language/Simile/ Metaphor
Amazing Bone, The William Steig Farrar, Straus and Giroux		Comprehension/Identify main ideas

BEFORE THE READ-ALOUD BEGINS

Previewing the Read-Aloud

Reading aloud is an art learned over time with lots of practice. To assure a smooth and enjoyable reading experience that also hits very clearly on the target standard, be sure to preview the book before you read it aloud to your students. Ideally, you'll consider the book's content and the scaffolds you may need to provide for your students' language and conceptual development. You may even want to slip in a few sticky notes to identify your stopping points—where you will pause to think aloud, guide a Thinking Partner conversation, or generate questions about the story. In this way, you'll consider both the instructional points you want to make and the magical moments you hope to create for your students. This preparation brings the intentionality that you apply in other areas of the curriculum into the heartbeat of your read-aloud, lifting the quality of the experience and increasing the instructional power.

Lester Laminack and Reba Wadsworth (2006) remind us that "when a read-aloud is done well, it is a performance; in our view, it is an art very akin to storytelling. The telling is as crucial to the listeners as is the tale" (p. 4).

> When you marry intentional, explicit teaching with the art of the read-aloud, you have a combination that is sure to delight, inform, and lift learners to new levels.

English Language Learners: Previewing and Scaffolding

Preview the mentor books with particular care to anticipate concepts that may be difficult or unfamiliar to your English language learners. During the preview, watch for cultural barriers that might inhibit understanding for a child learning a new language and a new culture. It is important to consider scaffolds, realia, and multicultural literature as additional supports.

Preparing the Shared Reading/Thinking and Readers Theater Segments

Every lesson contains both a text for shared reading/thinking and a Readers Theater script. These "Share the Learning" activities require that students be able to see the same text at the same time. You will want to make a transparency of the Share the Reading/Thinking page and display it on an overhead projector. You will notice that the text is enlarged as it is essential that students can easily see the text so they can participate in the shared reading and conversation.

Readers Theater requires that every student has his or her own copy of the script, so you will need to photocopy the scripts that are provided with each lesson or print them from the *Printable Resources* CD-ROM. Learners will use these scripts to practice and perform the selection. You—or the performers themselves—may want to highlight their roles on the script to make an actor's lines easy to locate. Students may also enjoy wearing a sign that labels the role they are reading or adding hats and other props to the performance.

Personalizing the Lessons

I encourage you to personalize the lessons by making connections to teaching points, favorite books, or shared experiences that you and your students can use to lift your thinking. I also encourage you to integrate your own favorite teaching strategies. Many teachers, for example, have students write on sticky notes during an interactive read-aloud and then use those sticky notes to support partner conversations and literature discussions. If that is a strategy that works for you, by all means add it! As you see in the following photos, pilot teacher Sherry Robertson followed the design of the mentor lesson, "Form Literal and Interpretive Questions," but added sticky notes so students could hold onto their questions through the conversations and writing that followed the lesson.

Interactive Read-Alouds *in Your Classroom*

Interactive Read-Alouds lessons do not provide a stand-alone program for your learners, nor are they simply "extras." They combine sparkling text and engaging conversations with truly deep and reflective thinking. The strategies that students learn during interactive read-alouds will allow them to successfully negotiate other classroom texts and the

texts of their lives. These standards-based lessons are rigorous, inviting, and effective for lifting students to higher levels of learning.

Thoughts from a Pilot Teacher

Leah Starkovich, Portland, Oregon

This new series is like one-stop shopping. Everything you need to teach a quality literature lesson is right at your fingertips. I am amazed at the conversations these lessons have generated in my classroom. This is a *fabulous resource for any teacher who enjoys teaching students to love books.*

INTERACTIVE READ-ALOUDS RESOURCES

This section includes an overview of program components, a lesson walkthrough, and a lesson planner that you can use to create your own interactive read-alouds.

Components

Each level of *Interactive Read-Alouds* provides

- the *Guide to Interactive Read-Alouds,* which outlines the thinking behind the lessons, offers practical classroom management advice, and contains forms for evaluating and tracking performance.
- the *Interactive Read-Alouds* lesson book, which is a collection of standards-based lessons built around children's classics. Shared reading/thinking texts and Readers Theater scripts for every lesson reinforce reading strategies and build oral fluency. The lesson walkthrough on the following pages highlights the instructional design of the lessons.
- a *Printable Resources* CD-ROM, which contains the shared reading/thinking texts and Readers Theater scripts from the lesson book as well as lesson planning, assessment, and tracking forms from this guide—all in an easily accessible PDF format.

Lesson Walkthrough

www.interactivereadalouds.com

MENTOR TEXT. A mentor text is an exemplary model of good literature and is the centerpiece of each lesson.

FOCUS STRATEGY/STANDARD. This is the instructional emphasis of the lesson.

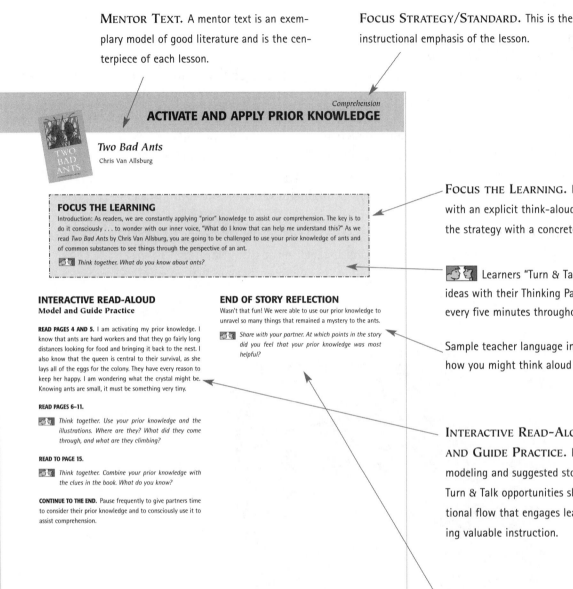

Comprehension
ACTIVATE AND APPLY PRIOR KNOWLEDGE

Two Bad Ants
Chris Van Allsburg

FOCUS THE LEARNING

Introduction: As readers, we are constantly applying "prior" knowledge to assist our comprehension. The key is to do it consciously . . . to wonder with our inner voice, "What do I know that can help me understand this?" As we read *Two Bad Ants* by Chris Van Allsburg, you are going to be challenged to use your prior knowledge of ants and of common substances to see things through the perspective of an ant.

Think together. What do you know about ants?

INTERACTIVE READ-ALOUD
Model and Guide Practice

READ PAGES 4 AND 5. I am activating my prior knowledge. I know that ants are hard workers and that they go fairly long distances looking for food and bringing it back to the nest. I also know that the queen is central to their survival, as she lays all of the eggs for the colony. They have every reason to keep her happy. I am wondering what the crystal might be. Knowing ants are small, it must be something very tiny.

READ PAGES 6–11.

Think together. Use your prior knowledge and the illustrations. Where are they? What did they come through, and what are they climbing?

READ TO PAGE 15.

Think together. Combine your prior knowledge with the clues in the book. What do you know?

CONTINUE TO THE END. Pause frequently to give partners time to consider their prior knowledge and to consciously use it to assist comprehension.

END OF STORY REFLECTION

Wasn't that fun! We were able to use our prior knowledge to unravel so many things that remained a mystery to the ants.

Share with your partner. At which points in the story did you feel that your prior knowledge was most helpful?

COMPREHENSION · 1

FOCUS THE LEARNING. Each lesson begins with an explicit think-aloud that introduces the strategy with a concrete example.

Learners "Turn & Talk," sharing their ideas with their Thinking Partners at least once every five minutes throughout the read-aloud.

Sample teacher language in each lesson shows how you might think aloud for your learners.

INTERACTIVE READ-ALOUD: MODEL AND GUIDE PRACTICE. Explicit teacher modeling and suggested stopping points for Turn & Talk opportunities show a clear instructional flow that engages learners while providing valuable instruction.

END OF STORY REFLECTION. The reflection after each read-aloud calls on students to revisit the standard and think explicitly about its application to reading.

TIP FOR SHARE THE READING/ THINKING. Tips for Share the Reading/Thinking provide ideas for using the new text with students. A full-size version of the text appears at the end of the lesson.

SHARE THE LEARNING. This two-part section includes tips and short shareable texts that invite students to practice and expand on the standard or skill they are learning.

TIP FOR READERS THEATER SCRIPT. The tips suggest ways of using the Readers Theater script that appears at the end of each lesson. From specific ideas for "performing" to enhance fluency and expressive reading to ideas for extensions, the tips allow you to customize for your learners' needs.

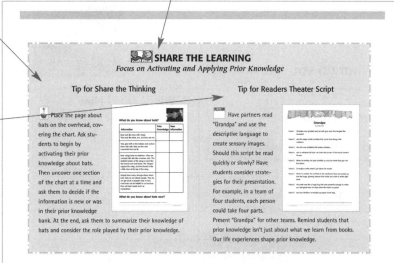

EXTEND THE LEARNING. Extension options suggest ways to hone your learners' thinking about strategies. Use the suggestions that best serve your students' needs.

ASSESS THE LEARNING. Assessment suggestions for each lesson provide ideas for ongoing assessment of strategy use. The assessment tools on pages 41–53 may be used to evaluate and record results of observations.

INFUSION OF FORMAL LANGUAGE: TEST-STYLE LANGUAGE. The two questions in each lesson expose students to the language of tests as they recall important ideas from the text.

What do you know about bats?

Information	Prior Knowledge	New Information
Bats look like mice with wings. They look like birds, too, but they are not.		
They give birth to live babies and nurture them with milk. Bats are the only mammals that can fly.		
Bats' wings have no feathers—they are covered with skin like a human arm. The skeletal system of the wing is much like the human arm and hand. The "fingers" support the wing, and the thumb is like a little claw at the top of the wing.		
People have many strange ideas about bats. Bats do not attack people. They do not get stuck in people's hair. In fact, most bats can be helpful to us because they eat insect pests such as mosquitoes.		

What do you know about bats now?

© 2007 by Linda Hoyt from *Interactive Read-Alouds, 4–5* (Portsmouth, NH: Heinemann). This page may be reproduced for classroom use only.

COMPREHENSION • 3

SHARED READING/THINKING OVERHEAD MASTER. The Share the Reading/Thinking text often introduces another genre for strategy practice. It provides an opportunity for you and the students to extend the strategy to new contexts and to read aloud together, building oral fluency. This full-size page may be made into an overhead transparency for group sharing and copied onto large charts. If you are keeping literacy notebooks with your students, they may want to include favorite lines from Share the Reading/Thinking selections.

READERS THEATER SCRIPT. Each lesson includes a Readers Theater script that provides an opportunity to develop oral fluency. The script may recap or use the same language structure as the mentor text, introduce a new genre (e.g., nonfiction), or extend the story context. Readers Theater fluency practice focuses on reading expressively and matching the reading to the purpose and type of text, and it should be joyous and engaging. Students should revel in the opportunity to show off their reading in a lively way.

Grandpa
by Linda Hoyt

Voice 1: Grandpa was grizzled and old with gray hair that tangled like seaweed

Voice 2: and the deep crinkly wrinkles that come from living a life outdoors.

Voice 3: His chin was stubbled with pokey whiskers,

Voice 4: and a withered old scar ran from the corner of his mouth toward his ear.

Voice 5: When he smiled, his eyes crinkled up and his whole face got into the action.

Voice 6: Grandpa's smile wasn't just about his mouth.

Voice 7: When he smiled, the wrinkles in his weathered face scrunched up into this huge, glowing beacon that made you want to smile right back.

Voice 8: His smile was like a huge hug that was powerful enough to make you feel good even on days when life wasn't so great

Voice 9: and you felt like a crumpled up paper lunch bag.

4 • COMPREHENSION

Lesson Planner for an Interactive Read-Aloud

The power of the interactive read-aloud is the ability to focus on a standard within an engaging text while challenging learners to think deeply. But are the texts included in this program the only possibilities for interactive read-alouds? Absolutely not! You can use any rich text that illustrates the concept or skill you want to focus on to craft an interactive read-aloud lesson.

> I am sure you have never done this, but I used to grab my read-aloud selections on my way past the bookshelf as I walked to the read-aloud area. I was convinced that any read-aloud was good...and I still think it is. However, why would we settle for just "good" when we can have great?
>
> —*Linda Hoyt*

Finding Read-Aloud Books

As we peruse our bookshelves, visit our local libraries, or check out catalogs of beautiful children's literature, we might ask of each title: Is there academic value? Will this read-aloud lift these students to a higher level of performance in any way? When read-alouds are understood as powerful tools for teaching literary elements, building analytical ability, and addressing the learning standards, they can bring both joy and accelerated learning into the lives of our students.

I have come to realize that I must take the work of selecting read-alouds very seriously. With the amazing array of quality children's literature available, we are selling ourselves and our students short if we settle for just any read-aloud. If we give it just a bit more thought and choose carefully, read-alouds can become a foundation for expansion of oral language, a challenging opportunity to stimulate deeper thinking, a rich moment when we can expose learners to beautiful art, and most certainly, a time when we can broaden students' world knowledge or focus on the craft of writing. The Lesson Matrix (pages 54–57) and the Title List (pages 58–72) will provide powerful support to your planning. The important thought here is to be intentional and explicit in your selections of books and your purposes.

Planning the Lesson

Once you've accomplished the most important task—choosing your mentor text—use the blank planner form on pages 37–38 to create your own interactive read-alouds. Following is a planner form annotated with notes on the kinds of thinking you'll want to put into planning an interactive read-aloud lesson. You can also download the Lesson Planner from the accompanying *Printable Resources* CD-ROM. Fill it in electronically, or print it out to fill in manually.

Lesson Planner (annotated)

MENTOR TEXT

Choose a text that is worthwhile, familiar, and available.

FOCUS STRATEGY/STANDARD

Choose one focus point that matches an important standard or learning goal in your classroom.

FOCUS THE LEARNING

Introduction: Identify a real-life example or an example that builds on a very familiar text to introduce the standard. Explain the standard in student-friendly terms, including precise vocabulary, e.g., *alliteration, prior knowledge, point of view*, and so on.

Turn & Talk: Provide a Turn & Talk prompt that focuses on the standard. Remember that you want a short burst (20–30 seconds) of focused talk not a long discussion.

INTERACTIVE READ-ALOUD: MODEL AND GUIDE PRACTICE

Cover: Note what you want to point out about the cover. Prepare a prompt to get students thinking about the cover and/or the standard.

Read to page _____.

Teacher think-aloud: Identify stopping points that make sense. You may stop several times throughout the reading of a text, or you may not stop at all! For each stopping point, plan an explicit think-aloud about the text and the standard. Use sticky notes to mark your stopping points.

Turn & Talk: Create a specific prompt or question that focuses students' attention on the standard and produces a brief partner exchange.

Read to page _____.

Teacher think-aloud: _____

_____

_____

Turn & Talk: _____

_____

---

continued

Lesson Planner (annotated), continued

Read to page _____.

Teacher think-aloud: _____

_____

_____

Turn & Talk: _____

_____

END OF STORY REFLECTION

Plan a reflection that models your thinking about the text and the standard. Craft a reflecting question for students

to ponder with a partner.

SHARE THE READING/THINKING

Learning Focus: Identify the standard being taught.

Text: Select a brief section from the mentor text. Prepare a visual to display to the group for shared

reading/thinking.

Ideas for Share the Reading/Thinking: Note ideas for providing continued experience with the standard.

READERS THEATER SCRIPT

Adapt a poem, lift a section of mentor text, or create your own Readers Theater script.

EXTEND THE LEARNING

List ideas for extending the learning. Consider ways to 1) apply the standard to other reading that you are doing;

2) apply the standard to a piece of writing that students are crafting or have already created; 3) extend the text,

keeping the standard in mind; and 4) introduce a new genre for learners to explore with the standard.

ASSESS THE LEARNING

List how you will assess students' use of the strategy. Consider 1) listening in as partners talk, 2) conferring during

independent reading and writing, and 3) using the assessment tools at the back of this guide.

Lesson Planner

MENTOR TEXT

_____

FOCUS STRATEGY/STANDARD

_____

_____

FOCUS THE LEARNING

Introduction: _____

_____

_____

Turn & Talk: _____

_____

INTERACTIVE READ-ALOUD: MODEL AND GUIDE PRACTICE

Cover: _____

_____

_____

Read to page _____.

Teacher think-aloud: _____

_____

_____

Turn & Talk: _____

_____

Read to page _____.

Teacher think-aloud: _____

_____

_____

Turn & Talk: _____

_____

continued

Lesson Planner, continued

Read to page _____.

Teacher think-aloud: _____

_____

_____

Turn & Talk: _____

_____

END OF STORY REFLECTION

_____

_____

SHARE THE READING/THINKING

Learning Focus: _____

Text: _____

_____

Ideas for Sharing the Reading/Thinking: _____

_____

READERS THEATER SCRIPT

_____

EXTEND THE LEARNING

_____

_____

_____

ASSESS THE LEARNING

_____

_____

_____

ASSESSMENT FORMS

Our primary purpose in assessing is to gather information about students' learning and inform our instruction. By using authentic assessment, we gain valuable insight into what students have learned and how they have learned it. We can plan instruction that will support those students who need additional support and challenge students who are ready to refine their use of strategies or move on to new ones. Not only does every read-aloud lesson in this collection provide specific suggestions for checking a learner's knowledge of the target standard, but also the entire lesson is a forum for observing and recording students' literacy behavior.

The following tools are designed to support ongoing multi-layered assessment. They can be used as they are, or you can use them as inspiration to create your own assessment tools. Most help you collect and keep data about individuals; many reflect change over time. For these, you'll need a copy of the form for each student you assess and a place to keep them until the next time you assess. You can use the scoring guide rubrics to assign grades, but more importantly, you can use them to have a "snapshot" of individuals and of your class as a whole. You will not want to use these tools on a daily basis but at intervals that are tied to your learning goals—when you have completed a cluster of read-alouds, for example, or when students have enough writing assignments to choose among for assessment with the help of a rubric. Three forms—Observation of Learners: READ-ALOUD, Observation of FLUENCY and EVALUATIVE RETELLING, and Teacher Record of INTERACTIVE READ-ALOUDS—help you compile information to assess group progress over time.

Observation of Learners: READ-ALOUD

Gather data during Interactive Read-Aloud *times. Tally as behavior is observed for each student.*

List names of students to the right.	Pays careful attention to think-alouds and reading selection.	Shifts purposefully from listening to partner conversation.	Offers eye contact and communication to partner.	Uses information gathered from the story and think-aloud in partner conversations.	Extends thinking with connections and questions.	Justifies opinions with evidence from text.	Summarizes story events (fiction).	Summarizes nonfiction selections and determines importance.	Infers.	Connects.	Generates main ideas.	Engages in sensory imaging.	Compares/contrasts.	Engages in evaluative analysis.	Describes elements of author's craft.	Identifies theme and author's purpose

Reader _____   Grade _____

Observation of ORAL LANGUAGE DEVELOPMENT

Gather data by listening to partner conversations during Interactive Read-Aloud *or while conferring during independent reading.*

	Date observed	Date observed	Date observed	Date observed
Speaks in complete, well-formed sentences.				
Demonstrates noun–verb agreement in oral speech.				
Supports opinions with evidence from a text.				
Asks for clarification when he or she doesn't understand.				
Retells a personal experience (includes *who, what, when, where*).				
Shifts language to match social setting (e.g., talking with friends vs. talking to principal).				
Responds appropriately to directions such as predict, identify, compare, analyze, evaluate, distinguish, and summarize.				
Notices when language is grammatically incorrect and tries again.				
Participates in conversation. Takes turns as speaker and listener.				
Uses language of abstract concepts, such as *love, hope, wish, what if, democratic,* and *fair*.				
Uses literary language (e.g., *once upon a time, character, setting, problem, solution*).				
Responds to multiple-meaning words with understanding.				
Uses connectives (*because, if, after, next, finally,* etc.).				
Makes connections linking learning with a prior experience or related reading.				
Delivers a concise, clear summary statement that includes main idea.				
Understands cause/effect and comparison.				
Uses descriptive language to help a listener visualize.				
Enunciates clearly and speaks at an understandable rate.				

Scoring Guide for FLUENCY and EXPRESSION

Gather data as part of **Share the Reading** *and* **Readers Theater** *interactions.*

Fluency refers to a reader's ability to interpret print through expressive oral reading. It is not just about "fast." It is about reading in a way that sounds like language and about representing the message of the author at a pace that matches the meaning. This means that the reader needs to pause in response to punctuation, phrasing, or powerful images and to select a pace that matches the kind of text and the purpose for the reading. With this in mind, a set of directions may be read very slowly as the reader concentrates on visualizing and internalizing the steps of a process, while a lively poem by Shel Silverstein may be read at a much faster pace as the language is savored and enjoyed.

(5) The reader reads with smoothness and expression.
The rate matches the kind of text being read.
The reader adjusts tone and emphasis to reflect meaning.
The reading reflects an understanding of audience.
Pauses are used for emphasis.
Punctuation is used to support expression.
Self-corrections and fix-up strategies are employed so smoothly that the listener does not notice them.

(3) There is some expressiveness in the reading.
There is some evidence of shifts in tone or inflection.
Reading is sometimes smooth and other times breaks down.
There is an attempt to match the rate to the kind of text being read.
The reader may over-exaggerate tone in an attempt to be dramatic.
The reader is so focused on print that the audience may be forgotten.
Pauses are focused on word recognition rather than emphasis of meaning.
Punctuation is sometimes used to support expressive interpretation.
Self-corrections and fix-up strategies are used but are obvious to a listener.

(1) The reader reads one word at a time.
There is little evidence of shifts in tone, speed, or inflection in response to meaning.
There are frequent pauses for sound-outs and repeats of words.
Time is taken to look at pictures to construct meaning.
The reader would benefit from more time to rehearse.

Adapted from *Snapshots: Literacy Minilessons Up Close*, Linda Hoyt, Heinemann, 2000.

Scoring Guide for EVALUATIVE RETELLING
Gather data after an Interactive Read-Aloud *by meeting with individuals.*

DIRECTIONS

Ask the student to look back through the pages of a book you have shared in read-aloud with the goal of preparing to *tell* what he or she learned from the book.

Meet with the student individually and encourage a complete evaluative retell with a cue such as: *Tell me about this book, especially those things that you think are the most important. Be sure to include your observations about theme, plot, and author's craft.*

Listen carefully. You may want to take notes. When the student finishes, you might want to offer additional encouragement with a cue such as one of the following:

1. *Is there anything else you can add?*

2. *If you were to recommend this book to someone, what might you say?*

3. *What were the strengths and weaknesses of this selection?*

RETELLING SCORING GUIDE

5 The learner states all main ideas and provides supporting details. Key concepts are clearly understood, and the learner offers opinions, makes connections, or makes a generalization. The learner explains with clarity and confidence. Opinions are supported with evidence, and observations about theme and craft are well articulated.

3 The learner states some main ideas and several supporting details. Most concepts are understood and expressed. The learner offers explanations that are grade-level appropriate. Events are described in sequence and opinions are offered, but theme and craft may not be thoroughly addressed.

1 The reader is not able to identify the main ideas. There may be a few details in the retell, but information is incomplete, inaccurate, or out of sequence. The reader may act hesitant and unsure. Opinions are not offered. Theme and craft are not addressed.

Observation of FLUENCY and EVALUATIVE RETELLING

DIRECTIONS

Insert scores from the Scoring Guides for Fluency and Evaluative Retelling into the chart below to track progress over time. Check "Fiction" or "Nonfiction," and be sure to gather data from both to get a broad overview of learner development.

Names	Observation 1 Date ___ ___Fiction ___Nonfiction		Observation 2 Date ___ ___Fiction ___Nonfiction		Observation 3 Date ___ ___Fiction ___Nonfiction		Observation 4 Date ___ ___Fiction ___Nonfiction	
	Fluency	Evaluative Retell	Fluency	Evaluative Retell	Fluency	Evaluative Retell	Fluency	Evaluative Retell

Scoring Guide for WRITING

	Just beginning (1) _____	The trait is developing (2) _____	Getting stronger (3) _____	Wow! (4) _____
Organization (the internal structure of the writing)	The picture carries much of the meaning, and the writing appears as labels on the picture or a single simple sentence. There is no distinct beginning or ending.	A beginning and ending are present but not well developed. There is more content but sequencing is not clear.	The beginning and ending are more interesting. Sequence is logical.	The beginning and ending are inviting and well-crafted. There is a clear sense of organization throughout the piece. Transitions link one section to another.
Content and Ideas (the meaning and core communication of the piece)	The writer has difficulty selecting a topic and offers few details.	A main idea is present, but there are few details and specifics.	Details are present and related to a broad topic. The writing is focused enough and rich enough in details to satisfy a reader's curiosity.	The topic is narrow and very well developed. Substantial detail is provided in a manner that interests the reader.
Voice (the writer's unique twist on communication; purpose and connection are evident)	The writer is not thinking about audience.	The writing is dull. It may feel formulaic or mechanical.	The writer is thinking about audience and has a clear purpose to the writing. The personality of the writer is beginning to show.	The writing is lively and draws in the reader. The writer's interest and connection to the topic show. There is a clear purpose and a sense of style.
Word Choice (rich vocabulary that adds detail and dimension)	Sentences are simple and not elaborated. Vocabulary is basic.	The writer uses functional words but seldom selects words that add interest and detail.	Verbs are becoming active and nouns more precise. Figurative language may be attempted.	Word choices show conscious thought about action in verbs and precision in nouns. Adjectives and figurative language create clear sensory images for the reader.
Sentence Fluency (the way words flow together from sentence to sentence)	Sentences do not flow together. The writing seems choppy and incomplete.	Sentences are of similar length, and many start in the same way.	Sentences have variety in length and in their beginnings. The piece can be read aloud comfortably.	There is a smooth flow to the writing. Sentences are varied and invite expressive oral reading.
Conventions (mechanics and technical aspects of the print)	Lack of conventional spelling affects readability.	Spelling is close to conventional and can be read. End punctuation and capitalization are used. Paragraphing may just be developing.	Spelling is strong. Grammar, punctuation, and paragraphing are close to conventional.	Spelling of even more difficult words tends to be correct. Punctuation includes commas and more sophisticated features.

Scoring Guide for WRITING, continued

	Just beginning (1) _____	The trait is developing (2) _____	Getting stronger (3) _____	Wow! (4) _____
Presentation (the visual appearance)	Handwriting is poor. Words are too close together. Messy appearance.	Spaces are provided between words. Appearance is better, but handwriting is still a challenge.	Spacing and handwriting are nicely done. Margins and overall appearance are neat and inviting.	Handwriting is uniform and well crafted. Space is used for text and for well-crafted visuals. Very inviting to the eye.
Text Features (the text and graphic features that support informational texts)	No text features are included in the writing.	Labels and a title are used.	Labels, title, boldface words, and captions are included in the writing.	Labels, title, boldface words, captions, close-up drawings, and cutaways are included in illustrations and supporting text.

Writer _____ Grade _____

Observation of WRITING

Evaluate writing and record scores based on the Scoring Guide for WRITING.

	Date _____ Score Observation #1	Date _____ Score Observation #2	Date _____ Score Observation #3	Date _____ Score Observation #4
Organization				
Content and Ideas				
Voice				
Word Choice				
Sentence Fluency				
Conventions				
Presentation				
Text Features				
OVERALL SCORE				

Student_____ Grade _____

EVIDENCE of LEARNING Checklist

Students should be able to explain the standard using specific references to a particular selection. It is important to find evidence of understanding in multiple contexts. When appropriate to the comprehension task, include fiction and nonfiction to ensure deep understanding. Gather data by listening to partner conversations in read aloud, during small group instruction, or in one to one reading conferences.

	Date Observed: _____	Date Observed: _____	Date Observed: _____	Implications for Instruction
	( ) Fiction ( ) Nonfiction	( ) Fiction ( ) Nonfiction	( ) Fiction ( ) Nonfiction	
Standards for Comprehension				
Activate and apply prior knowledge				
Form literal and interpretive questions				
Make connections				
Connect to culture/experiences of others				
Analyze critically				
Interpret				
Construct sensory images				
Infer				
Draw and support conclusions				
Compare/Contrast				
Identify cause and effect				
Identify main ideas				
Determine importance				
Determine purpose				
Represent text with an organizer				
Summarize				
Standards for Structural Elements				
Plot				
Problem/Solution structure				
Illustration				
Climax				
Main idea				
Setting				
Character development				
Theme				
Dialogue				
Tone/Mood				

EVIDENCE of LEARNING Checklist, continued

	Date Observed: _____ () Fiction () Nonfiction	Date Observed: _____ () Fiction () Nonfiction	Date Observed: _____ () Fiction () Nonfiction	Implications for Instruction
Standards for Vocabulary/ Literary Language				
Precise vocabulary				
Word meanings				
Literary/Figurative language				
Alliteration				
Onomatopoeia				
Simile/Metaphor				
Repetition				
Transition words				
Standards for Literary Elements and Devices				
Point of view				
Personification				
Foreshadowing				
Flashback				
Allusion				
Symbolism				
Hyperbole/Obvious exaggeration				
Imagery				
Poetic justice				
Irony				
Standards for Genre				
Distinguishing features of fiction				
Distinguishing features of nonfiction				
Biography				
Historical fiction				
Fairy Tale/Folktale/Tall tale				
Fantasy				
Poetry				
Standards for Writing Traits				
Ideas				
Organization				
Voice				
Word choice				
Sentence fluency				
Conventions				

Teacher Record of INTERACTIVE READ-ALOUDS

Keep track of the standards you address and the books you pair with each standard.

COMPREHENSION					
Standard	Date/Title	Date/Title	Date/Title	Date/Title	Date/Title
Activate and apply prior knowledge					
Form literal and interpretive questions					
Make connections					
Connect to the culture/experiences of others					
Analyze critically					
Interpret					
Construct sensory images					
Infer					
Draw and support conclusions					
Compare/Contrast					
Identify cause and effect					
Identify main ideas					
Determine importance					
Determine purpose					
Represent text with an organizer					
Summarize					

continued

Teacher Record of INTERACTIVE READ-ALOUDS, continued

STRUCTURAL ELEMENTS					
Standard	Date/Title	Date/Title	Date/Title	Date/Title	Date/Title
Plot					
Problem/Solution structure					
Illustration					
Climax					
Main idea					
Setting					
Character development					
Theme					
Dialogue					
Tone/Mood					

VOCABULARY/LITERARY LANGUAGE					
Standard	Date/Title	Date/Title	Date/Title	Date/Title	Date/Title
Precise vocabulary					
Word meanings					
Literary/Figurative language					
Alliteration					
Onomatopoeia					
Simile/Metaphor					
Repetition					
Transition words					

Teacher Record of INTERACTIVE READ-ALOUDS, continued

LITERARY ELEMENTS AND DEVICES					
Standard	Date/Title	Date/Title	Date/Title	Date/Title	Date/Title
Point of view					
Personification					
Foreshadowing					
Flashback					
Allusion					
Symbolism					
Hyperbole/Obvious exagggeration					
Imagery					
Poetic justice					
Irony					

GENRE					
Standard	Date/Title	Date/Title	Date/Title	Date/Title	Date/Title
Distinguishing features of fiction					
Distinguishing features of nonfiction					
Biography					
Historical fiction					
Fairy tale/Folktale/Tall tale					
Fantasy					
Poetry					

WRITING TRAITS					
Standard	Date/Title	Date/Title	Date/Title	Date/Title	Date/Title
Ideas					
Organization					
Voice					
Word choice					
Sentence fluency					
Conventions					

LESSON MATRIX

This chart identifies the mentor text used in the model lesson for each standard. (Standards for Writing Traits have two mentor texts and model lessons.) Booklinks are other wonderful books that help students expand and practice the standard. Use the lesson planner provided in this guide and on the *Printable Resources* CD-ROM to create your own lessons using the Booklinks.

LESSON MATRIX							
Standards for COMPREHENSION							
Page Ref	**Standard**	**4/5 Mentor Text**	**Booklink 1**	**Booklink 2**	**Booklink 3**	**Booklink 4**	**Booklink 5**
1	Activate and apply prior knowledge	*Two Bad Ants*	More Than Anything Else	Wall, The	Martin's Big Words	Yellow Star, The	Number the Stars
7	Form literal and interpretive questions	*Cheyenne Again*	Faithful Elephants	Passage to Freedom	Mysteries of Harris Burdick, The	Wilma Unlimited	Sign of the Beaver
13	Make connections	*Dandelions*	Ox-Cart Man	Thank You, Mr. Falker	Dakota Dugout	Train to Somewhere, The	Stone Fox
19	Connect to the culture/ experiences of others	*Annie and the Old One*	So Far from the Sea	Black Whiteness	Knots on a Counting Rope	All the Places to Love	Bud, Not Buddy
25	Analyze critically	*Yellow Star, The*	Table Where Rich People Sit, The	So You Want to Be President?	Faithful Elephants	Man Who Walked Between the Towers, The	Number the Stars
31	Interpret	*Mysteries of Harris Burdick, The*	Snowflake Bentley	Grandfather's Journey	Mirandy and Brother Wind	Girl Who Loved Wild Horses, The	Giver, The
35	Construct sensory images	*Dogteam*	Great Kapok Tree, The	Black Whiteness	Snowflake Bentley	Charlotte's Web	Tale of Despereaux, The
41	Infer	*Gardener, The*	Two Bad Ants	Smoky Night	Van Gogh Café, The	So You Want to Be President?	Shiloh
47	Draw and support conclusions	*Smoky Night*	Freedom Summer	Seven Blind Mice	Gleam and Glow	Brother Eagle, Sister Sky	Maniac Magee
51	Compare/Contrast	*Butterfly, The and Gleam and Glow*	Black and White	Martin's Big Words and My Brother Martin	Dogteam and Owl Moon	So You Want to Be President?	Sarah, Plain and Tall and Dandelions
57	Identify cause and effect	*True Story of the Three Little Pigs, The*	Other Side, The	Faithful Elephants	Gardener, The	Mufaro's Beautiful Daughters	Julie of the Wolves
63	Identify main ideas	*So You Want to be President?*	Gardener, The	Amazing Bone, The	Martin's Big Words	Snowflake Bentley	Summer of the Swans
69	Determine importance	*Snowflake Bentley*	Passage to Freedom	Grandfather's Journey	Black Whiteness	Smoky Night	Onion John
75	Determine purpose	*Joyful Noise*	Wall, The	Drop of Water, A	Pink and Say	Man Who Walked Between the Towers, The	Lincoln: A Photobiography
81	Represent text with an organizer	*Drop of Water, A*	Dinosaurs of Waterhouse Hawkins, The	Faithful Friend, The	Sweet Clara and the Freedom Quilt	Casey at the Bat	Whipping Boy, The
87	Summarize	*Chicken Sunday*	Snowflake Bentley	Ox-Cart Man	Lincoln: A Photobiography	So Far from the Sea	Wrinkle in Time, A

continued

LESSON MATRIX

Standards for STRUCTURAL ELEMENTS

Page Ref	Standard	4/5 Mentor Text	Booklink 1	Booklink 2	Booklink 3	Booklink 4	Booklink 5
93	Plot	*Mufaro's Beautiful Daughters*	Grandfather's Journey	Duke Ellington	Sweet Clara and the Freedom Quilt	St. George and the Dragon	Hatchet
99	Problem/Solution structure	*Jumanji*	Chicken Sunday	Lon Po Po	Two Bad Ants	Wilma Unlimited	Where the Red Fern Grows
105	Illustration	*Owl Moon*	Smoky Night	Tuesday	Girl Who Loved Wild Horses, The	Seven Blind Mice	Lincoln: A Photobiography
111	Climax	*Pink and Say*	Casey at the Bat	Yellow Star, The	Thank You, Mr. Falker	Gleam and Glow	Bridge to Terabithia
117	Main idea	*When I Was Young in the Mountains*	Girl Who Loved Wild Horses, The	Wilma Unlimited	Great Kapok Tree, The	Important Book, The	Number the Stars
123	Setting	*Two Bad Ants*	So Far from the Sea	Black Whiteness	When I Was Young in the Mountains	Harlem	Charlotte's Web
129	Character development	*Snowflake Bentley*	Faithful Friend, The	Martin's Big Words	Gardener, The	Sarah, Plain and Tall	Tales of a Fourth Grade Nothing
135	Theme	*Other Side, The*	So Far from the Sea	Table Where Rich People Sit, The	Faithful Elephants	Librarian of Basra, The	Tuck Everlasting
141	Dialogue	*True Story of the Three Little Pigs, The*	Mirandy and Brother Wind	Sweet Clara and the Freedom Quilt	Chicken Sunday	Tough Cookie	Indian in the Cupboard, The
147	Tone/Mood	*Cheyenne Again*	True Story of the Three Little Pigs, The	Thank You, Mr. Falker	Yo, Hungry Wolf!	So You Want to Be President?	Wayside School Is Falling Down

Standards for VOCABULARY/LITERARY LANGUAGE

Page Ref	Standard	4/5 Mentor Text	Booklink 1	Booklink 2	Booklink 3	Booklink 4	Booklink 5
151	Precise vocabulary	*Drop of Water, A*	Annie and the Old One	Under the Quilt of Night	Owl Moon	Dogteam	Tuck Everlasting; View from Saturday, The
155	Word meanings	*Miss Alaineus*	True Story of the Three Little Pigs, The	King Who Rained, The	Chocolate Moose for Dinner, A	Sylvester and the Magic Pebble	Series of Unfortunate Events, A
161	Literary/Figurative language	*Home Run*	Owl Moon	St. George and the Dragon	Mirandy and Brother Wind (dialect)	Snowflake Bentley	Tuck Everlasting
167	Alliteration	*Z Was Zapped, The*	Miss Alaineus	Harlem	How the Grinch Stole Christmas	Shrek!	Animalia
171	Onomatopoeia	*Sector 7*	Home Run	How the Grinch Stole Christmas	Three Pigs, The	Sky Dogs	Love That Dog
177	Simile/Metaphor	*Tar Beach*	Tough Cookie	Snowflake Bentley	If Not for the Cat	All the Places to Love	Pictures of Hollis Woods
183	Repetition	*Alexander and the Terrible, Horrible, No Good, Very Bad Day*	When I Was Young in the Mountains	Dogteam	If I Were in Charge of the World	Click, Clack, Moo	Great Gilly Hopkins, The
187	Transition words	*Wilma Unlimited*	Chicken Sunday	Drummer Boy	Animals Nobody Loves	Where the Sidewalk Ends, "True Story"	Stone Fox

continued

LESSON MATRIX

Standards for LITERARY ELEMENTS AND DEVICES

Page Ref	Standard	4/5 Mentor Text	Booklink 1	Booklink 2	Booklink 3	Booklink 4	Booklink 5
193	Point of view	*So Far from the Sea*	Two Bad Ants	True Story of the Three Little Pigs, The	Faithful Elephants	Tough Cookie	Pictures of Hollis Woods
197	Personification	*Heartland*	True Story of the Three Little Pigs, The	Mirandy and Brother Wind	Tough Cookie	Frog Prince Continued, The	Tale of Despereaux, The
203	Foreshadowing	*Yellow Star, The*	Grandfather's Journey	How Many Days to America?	Passage to Freedom	Table Where Rich People Sit, The	Sign of the Beaver
209	Flashback	*Wreck of the Zephyr, The*	Dinosaurs of Waterhouse Hawkins, The	Keeping Quilt, The	Nettie's Trip South	Home Place	Lion, the Witch and the Wardrobe, The
215	Allusion	*Tough Cookie*	Tar Beach	Fairytale News	Stinky Cheese Man and Other Fairly Stupid Tales, The	Three Little Wolves and the Big Bad Pig	Sleeping Ugly
221	Symbolism	*Barefoot*	Butterfly, The	Tar Beach	Gleam and Glow	Giving Tree, The	Lion, the Witch and the Wardrobe, The
227	Hyperbole/Obvious exaggeration	*Piggy Pie!*	Library Lil	Bunyans, The	Heat Wave	Cloudy with a Chance of Meatballs	Shrek!
233	Imagery	*Owl Moon*	Sylvester and the Magic Pebble	If Not for the Cat	Harlem	Home Place	Golem
239	Poetic justice	*Widow's Broom, The*	Quicksand Book, The	Grizz	Sweetest Fig, The	Why Mosquitoes Buzz in People's Ears	Holes
245	Irony	*Frog Prince Continued, The*	Table Where Rich People Sit, The	Yellow Star, The	Sweetest Fig, The	Golem	Angel for Solomon Singer, An

Standards for GENRE

Page Ref	Standard	4/5 Mentor Text	Booklink 1	Booklink 2	Booklink 3	Booklink 4	Booklink 5
251	Distinguishing features of fiction	*Chicken Sunday; Pink and Say; Jumanji, Black and White; Rumpelstiltskin; Girl Who Loved Wild Horses, The*	Fables	Gardener, The	Stranger, The	Sector 7	Westing Game, The
257	Distinguishing features of nonfiction	*Dinosaurs of Waterhouse Hawkins, The; Drop of Water, A*	Animals Nobody Loves	Caves	So You Want to Be President?	Heart, The	Immigrant Kids
263	Biography	*Martin's Big Words*	Home Run	Wilma Unlimited	Snowflake Bentley	Dinosaurs of Waterhouse Hawkins, The	Through My Eyes (autobiography)
269	Historical fiction	*Dakota Dugout*	Under the Quilt of Night	Gardener, The	Faithful Elephants	Sweet Clara and the Freedom Quilt	Sadako and the Thousand Paper Cranes

continued

Standards for GENRE, *continued*

Page Ref	Standard	4/5 Mentor Text	Booklink 1	Booklink 2	Booklink 3	Booklink 4	Booklink 5
275	Fairy tale/Folktale Tall tale	*Rumpelstiltskin*	Story of Jumping Mouse, The (folktale)	Bunyans, The (tall tale)	Little Red Riding Hood	Ugly Duckling, The	Tale of Despereaux, The
281	Fantasy	*Tuesday*	Stranger, The	Baloney (Henry P.)	Sector 7	Three Pigs, The	Harry Potter and the Sorcerer's Stone
287	Poetry	*Casey at the Bat*	If Not for the Cat	Where the Sidewalk Ends	Joyful Noise	Under the Quilt of Night	Love That Dog

Standards for WRITING TRAITS

Page Ref	Standard	4/5 Mentor Text	4/5 Mentor Text	Booklink 2	Booklink 3	Booklink 4	Booklink 5
293	Ideas	*Home Run*	*Nothing Ever Happens on 90th Street*	Heartland	Important Book, The	I'm in Charge of Celebrations	Kira-Kira
307	Organization	*Lincoln: A Photobiography*	*Z Was Zapped, The*	Ashanti to Zulu	Dogteam	Wilma Unlimited	Because of Winn-Dixie
321	Voice	*Under the Quilt of Night*	*If I Were in Charge of the World*	Diary of a Worm	Harlem	Piggy Pie!	On My Honor
333	Word choice	*Caves*	*Owl Moon*	Amos and Boris	Under the Quilt of Night	If Not for the Cat	Series of Unfortunate Events, A
347	Sentence fluency	*All the Places to Love*	*Important Book, The*	Oh, the Places You'll Go!	Harlem	Owl Moon	Out of the Dust
359	Conventions	*Punctuation Takes a Vacation*	*Heart, The*	Yo! Yes?	Kites Sail High	Hooray for Diffendoofer Day!	Frindle

TITLE LIST

This chart will help you locate lessons that fit each title. "Mentor Lessons" use the title as a mentor text. "Booklinks" list standards for which the title is an excellent extension text. Use the lesson planner on pages 37–38 in *Guide to Interactive Read-Alouds* or on the *Printable Resources* CD-ROM to create lessons for Booklinks. "Strand" identifies the tabbed section in which you will find each lesson in the lesson book. "Standard" identifies the lesson's focus.

TITLE LIST		
Book Title, Author, and Publisher	**Mentor Lessons** **Strand/Standard**	**Booklinks** **Strand/Standard**
Alexander and the Terrible, Horrible, No Good, ***Very Bad Day*** Judith Viorst Atheneum	Vocabulary/Literary Language/Repetition Comprehension/Determine purpose	
All the Places to Love Patricia MacLachlan Joanna Cotler	Writing Traits/Sentence fluency	Comprehension/Connect to the culture/ experiences of others Vocabulary/Literary Language/Simile/ Metaphor
Amazing Bone, The William Steig Farrar, Straus and Giroux		Comprehension/Identify main ideas
Amos and Boris William Steig Farrar, Straus and Giroux		Writing Traits/Word choice
Angel for Solomon Singer, An Cynthia Rylant Scholastic		Literary Elements and Devices/Irony
Animalia Graeme Base Harry N. Abrams		Vocabulary/Literary Language/Alliteration
Animals Nobody Loves Seymour Simon SeaStar		Vocabulary/Literary Language/Transition words Genre/Distinguishing features of nonfiction
Annie and the Old One Miska Miles Little, Brown Young Readers	Comprehension/Connect to the culture/ experiences of others	Vocabulary/Literary Language/ Precise vocabulary
Ashanti to Zulu Margaret Musgrove Dial		Writing Traits/Organization

TITLE LIST		
Book Title, Author, and Publisher	**Mentor Lessons** **Strand/Standard**	**Booklinks** **Strand/Standard**
Baloney (Henry P.) Jon Scieszka Puffin		Genre/Fantasy
Barefoot Pamela Duncan Edwards Scholastic	Literary Elements and Devices/Symbolism	
Because of Winn-Dixie Kate DiCamillo Candlewick		Writing Traits/Organization
Black and White David Macaulay Houghton Mifflin	Genre/Distinguishing features of fiction	Comprehension/Compare/Contrast
Black Whiteness Robert Burleigh Atheneum		Comprehension/Connect to the culture/ experiences of others Comprehension/Construct sensory images Comprehension/Determine importance Structural Elements/Setting
Bridge to Terabithia Katherine Paterson HarperCollins		Structural Elements/Climax
Brother Eagle, Sister Sky Susan Jeffers Dial		Comprehension/Draw and support conclusions
Bud, Not Buddy Christopher Paul Curtis Delacorte		Comprehension/Connect to the culture/ experiences of others
Bunyans, The Audrey Wood Blue Sky Press		Literary Elements and Devices/Hyperbole/Obvious exaggeration Genre/Fairy tale/Folktale/Tall tale
Butterfly, The Patricia Polacco Philomel	Comprehension/Compare/Contrast Comprehension/Determine purpose	Literary Elements and Devices/Symbolism
Casey at the Bat Ernest L. Thayer Putnam Juvenile	Genre/Poetry	Comprehension/Represent text with an organizer Structural Elements/Climax
Caves Stephen P. Kramer Carolrhoda Books	Writing Traits/Word choice	Genre/Distinguishing features of nonfiction

	TITLE LIST	
Book Title, Author, and Publisher	**Mentor Lessons** **Strand/Standard**	**Booklinks** **Strand/Standard**
Charlotte's Web E. B. White HarperCollins		Comprehension/Construct sensory images Structural Elements/Setting
Cheyenne Again Eve Bunting Clarion Books	Comprehension/Form literal and interpretive questions Structural Elements/Tone/Mood	
Chicken Sunday Patricia Polacco Philomel	Comprehension/Summarize Genre/Distinguishing features of fiction	Structural Elements/Problem/Solution structure Structural Elements/Dialogue Vocabulary/Literary Language/Transition words
Chocolate Moose for Dinner, A Fred Gwynne Aladdin		Vocabulary/Literary Language/ Word meanings
Click, Clack, Moo: Cows That Type Doreen Cronin Simon & Schuster		Vocabulary/Literary Language/Repetition
Cloudy with a Chance of Meatballs Judi Barrett Atheneum		Literary Elements and Devices/Hyperbole/Obvious exaggeration
Dakota Dugout Ann Turner Simon & Schuster	Genre/Historical fiction	Comprehension/Make connections
Dandelions Eve Bunting Harcourt	Comprehension/Make connections Genre/Historical fiction	Comprehension/Compare/Contrast
Diary of a Worm Doreen Cronin Joanna Cotler		Writing Traits/Voice
Dinosaurs of Waterhouse Hawkins, The Barbara Kerley Scholastic	Genre/Distinguishing features of nonfiction	Comprehension/Represent text with an organizer Literary Elements and Devices/Flashback Genre/Biography
Dogteam Gary Paulsen Bantam	Comprehension/Construct sensory images	Comprehension/Compare/Contrast Vocabulary/Literary Language/Precise vocabulary Vocabulary/Literary Language/Repetition Writing Traits/Organization

	TITLE LIST	
Book Title, Author, and Publisher	**Mentor Lessons** **Strand/Standard**	**Booklinks** **Strand/Standard**
Drop of Water, A Walter Wick Scholastic	Comprehension/Represent text with an organizer Vocabulary/Literary Language/Precise vocabulary Genre/Distinguishing features of nonfiction	Comprehension/Determine purpose
Drummer Boy Ann Turner HarperCollins		Vocabulary/Literary Language/Transition words
Duke Ellington Andrea Davis Pinkney Jump at the Sun		Structural Elements/Plot
Fables Arnold Lobel HarperCollins		Genre/Distinguishing features of fiction
Fairytale News Colin and Jacqui Hawkins Candlewick		Literary Elements and Devices/Allusion
Faithful Elephants Yukio Tsuchiya Houghton Mifflin		Comprehension/Form literal and interpretive questions Comprehension/Analyze critically Comprehension/Identify cause and effect Structural Elements/Theme Literary Elements and Devices/Point of view Genre/Historical fiction
Faithful Friend, The Robert D. San Souci Aladdin		Comprehension/Represent text with an organizer Structural Elements/Character development
Freedom Summer Deborah Wiles Atheneum/Ann Schwartz Books		Comprehension/Draw and support conclusions
Frindle Andrew Clements Simon & Schuster		Writing Traits/Conventions
Frog Prince Continued, The Jon Scieszka Puffin	Literary Elements and Devices/Irony	Literary Elements and Devices/Personification

TITLE LIST

Book Title, Author, and Publisher	Mentor Lessons Strand/Standard	Booklinks Strand/Standard
Gardener, The Sarah Stewart Farrar, Straus & Giroux	Comprehension/Infer	Comprehension/Identify cause and effect Comprehension/Identify main ideas Structural Elements/Character development Genre/Distinguishing features of fiction Genre/Historical fiction
Girl Who Loved Wild Horses, The Paul Goble Atheneum	Genre/Distinguishing features of fiction	Comprehension/Interpret Structural Elements/Illustration Structural Elements/Main idea
Giver, The Lois Lowry Houghton Mifflin		Comprehension/Interpret
Giving Tree, The Shel Silverstein HarperCollins		Literary Elements and Devices/Symbolism
Gleam and Glow Eve Bunting Harcourt	Comprehension/Compare/Contrast	Comprehension/Draw and support conclusions Structural Elements/Climax Literary Elements and Devices/Symbolism
Golem David Wisniewski Clarion		Literary Elements and Devices/Imagery Literary Elements and Devices/Irony
Grandfather's Journey Allen Say Houghton Mifflin		Comprehension/Interpret Comprehension/Determine importance Structural Elements/Plot Literary Elements and Devices/Foreshadowing
Great Gilly Hopkins, The Katherine Paterson HarperCollins		Vocabulary/Literary Language/Repetition
Great Kapok Tree, The Lynne Cherry Gulliver Green		Comprehension/Construct sensory images Structural Elements/Main idea
Grizz Eric Kimmel Holiday House		Literary Elements and Devices/Poetic justice
Harlem Walter Dean Myers Scholastic		Structural Elements/Setting Vocabulary/Literary Language/Alliteration Literary Elements and Devices/Imagery Writing Traits/Voice Writing Traits/Sentence fluency

Book Title, Author, and Publisher	Mentor Lessons Strand/Standard	Booklinks Strand/Standard
Harry Potter and the Sorcerer's Stone J. K. Rowling Arthur A. Levine		Genre/Fantasy
Hatchet Gary Paulsen Atheneum		Structural Elements/Plot
Heart, The Seymour Simon HarperCollins	Writing Traits/Conventions	Genre/Distinguishing features of nonfiction
Heartland Diane Siebert HarperCollins	Literary Elements and Devices/Personification	Writing Traits/Ideas
Heat Wave Helen Ketteman Walker & Company		Literary Elements and Devices/Hyperbole/Obvious exaggeration
Holes Louis Sachar Farrar, Straus & Giroux		Literary Elements and Devices/Poetic justice
Home Place Crescent Dragonwagon Atheneum		Literary Elements and Devices/Flashback Literary Elements and Devices/Imagery
Home Run Robert Burleigh Silver Whistle	Vocabulary/Literary Language/Literary/Figurative language Writing Traits/Ideas	Vocabulary/Literary Language/Onomatopoeia Genre/Biography
Hooray for Diffendoofer Day! Dr. Seuss Knopf		Writing Traits/Conventions
How Many Days to America? Eve Bunting Clarion		Literary Elements and Devices/Foreshadowing
How the Grinch Stole Christmas Dr. Seuss Random House		Vocabulary/Literary Language/Alliteration Vocabulary/Literary Language/Onomatopoeia
I'm in Charge of Celebrations Byrd Baylor Aladdin		Writing Traits/Ideas

	TITLE LIST	
Book Title, Author, and Publisher	**Mentor Lessons** Strand/Standard	**Booklinks** Strand/Standard
If I Were in Charge of the World Judith Viorst Atheneum	Writing Traits/Voice	Vocabulary/Literary Language/Repetition
If Not for the Cat Jack Prelutsky Greenwillow		Vocabulary/Literary Language/Simile/ Metaphor Literary Elements and Devices/Imagery Genre/Poetry Writing Traits/Word choice
Immigrant Kids Russell Freedman Dutton		Genre/Distinguishing features of nonfiction
Important Book, The Margaret Wise Brown HarperTrophy	Writing Traits/Sentence fluency	Structural Elements/Main idea Writing Traits/Ideas
Indian in the Cupboard, The Lynne Reid Banks Doubleday		Structural Elements/Dialogue
Joyful Noise Paul Fleischman HarperTrophy	Comprehension/Determine purpose	Genre/Poetry
Julie of the Wolves Jean Craighead George HarperCollins		Comprehension/Identify cause and effect
Jumanji Chris Van Allsburg Houghton Mifflin	Structural Elements/Problem/Solution structure Genre/Distinguishing features of fiction	
Keeping Quilt, The Patricia Polacco Simon & Schuster		Literary Elements and Devices/Flashback
King Who Rained, The Fred Gwynne Aladdin		Vocabulary/Literary Language/ Word meanings
Kira-Kira Cynthia Kadohata Atheneum		Writing Traits/Ideas
Kites Sail High Ruth Heller Putnam		Writing Traits/Conventions

Book Title, Author, and Publisher	Mentor Lessons Strand/Standard	Booklinks Strand/Standard
Knots on a Counting Rope Bill Martin, Jr., and John Archambault Henry Holt and Co.		Comprehension/Connect to the culture/ experiences of others
Librarian of Basra, The Jeanette Winter Harcourt		Structural Elements/Theme
Library Lil Suzanne Williams Dial		Literary Elements and Devices/Hyperbole/ Obvious exaggeration
Lincoln: A Photobiography Russell Freedman Clarion	Writing Traits/Organization	Comprehension/Determine purpose Comprehension/Summarize Structural Elements/Illustration
Lion, the Witch and the Wardrobe, The C. S. Lewis HarperCollins		Literary Elements and Devices/Flashback Literary Elements and Devices/Symbolism
Little Red Riding Hood Trina Schart Hyman Holiday House		Genre/Fairy tale/Folktale/Tall tale
Lon Po Po Ed Young Philomel		Structural Elements/Problem/Solution structure
Love That Dog Sharon Creech Joanna Cotler		Vocabulary/Literary Language/Onomatopoeia Genre/Poetry
Man Who Walked Between the Towers, The Mordicai Gerstein Roaring Brook Press/Millbrook Press		Comprehension/Analyze critically Comprehension/Determine purpose
Maniac Magee Jerry Spinelli Little, Brown		Comprehension/Draw and support conclusions
Martin's Big Words Doreen Rapport Jump at the Sun/Hyperion	Genre/Biography	Comprehension/Activate and apply prior knowledge Comprehension/Compare/Contrast Comprehension/Identify main ideas Structural Elements/Character development
Mirandy and Brother Wind Patricia C. McKissack Knopf		Comprehension/Interpret Structural Elements/Dialogue Vocabulary/Literary Language/Literary/ Figurative language (dialect) Literary Elements and Devices/Personification

	TITLE LIST	
Book Title, Author, and Publisher	**Mentor Lessons** **Strand/Standard**	**Booklinks** **Strand/Standard**
Miss Alaineus Debra Frasier Harcourt	Vocabulary/Literary Language/ Word meanings	Vocabulary/Literary Language/Alliteration
More Than Anything Else Marie Bradby Scholastic		Comprehension/Activate and apply prior knowledge
Mufaro's Beautiful Daughters John Steptoe Lothrop	Structural Elements/Plot	Comprehension/Identify cause and effect
My Brother Martin Christine King Farris Simon & Schuster	Genre/Biography	Comprehension/Compare/Contrast
Mysteries of Harris Burdick, The Chris Van Allsburg Houghton Mifflin	Comprehension/Interpret	Comprehension/Form literal and interpretive questions
Nettie's Trip South Ann Turner Macmillan		Literary Elements and Devices/Flashback
Nothing Ever Happens on 90th Street Roni Schotter Scholastic	Writing Traits/Ideas	
Number the Stars Lois Lowry Houghton Mifflin		Comprehension/Activate and apply prior knowledge Comprehension/Analyze critically Structural Elements/Main idea
Oh, the Places You'll Go! Dr. Seuss Random House		Writing Traits/Sentence fluency
On My Honor Marion Dane Bauer Clarion		Writing Traits/Voice
Onion John Joseph Krumgold Crowell		Comprehension/Determine importance
Other Side, The Jacqueline Woodson Putnam	Structural Elements/Theme	Comprehension/Identify cause and effect

TITLE LIST

Book Title, Author, and Publisher	Mentor Lessons Strand/Standard	Booklinks Strand/Standard
Out of the Dust Karen Hesse Scholastic		Writing Traits/Sentence fluency
Owl Moon Jane Yolen Philomel	Structural Elements/Illustration Literary Elements and Devices/Imagery Writing Traits/Word choice	Comprehension/Compare/Contrast Vocabulary/Literary Language/Precise vocabulary Vocabulary/Literary Language/Literary/ Figurative language Writing Traits/Sentence fluency
Ox-Cart Man Donald Hall Viking		Comprehension/Make connections Comprehension/Summarize
Passage to Freedom Ken Mochizuki Lee & Low Books		Comprehension/Form literal and interpretive questions Comprehension/Determine importance Literary Elements and Devices/Foreshadowing
Pictures of Hollis Woods Patricia Reilly Giff Wendy Lamb Books		Vocabulary/Literary Language/Simile/Metaphor Literary Elements and Devices/Point of view
Piggy Pie! Margie Palatini Clarion	Literary Elements and Devices/ Hyperbole/Obvious exaggeration	Writing Traits/Voice
Pink and Say Patricia Polacco Philomel	Structural Elements/Climax Genre/Distinguishing features of fiction	Comprehension/Determine purpose
Punctuation Takes a Vacation Robin Pulver Holiday House	Writing Traits/Conventions	
Quicksand Book, The Tomie dePaola Holiday House		Literary Elements and Devices/Poetic justice
Rumpelstiltskin Paul O. Zelinsky Dutton	Genre/Distinguishing features of fiction Genre/Fairy tale/Folktale/Tall tale	
Sadako and the Thousand Paper Cranes Eleanor Coerr Putnam		Genre/Historical fiction

TITLE LIST		
Book Title, Author, and Publisher	Mentor Lessons Strand/Standard	Booklinks Strand/Standard
Sarah, Plain and Tall Patricia MacLachlan HarperTrophy		Comprehension/Compare/Contrast Structural Elements/Character development
Sector 7 David Wiesner Clarion	Vocabulary/Literary Language/ Onomatopoeia	Genre/Distinguishing features of fiction Genre/Fantasy
Series of Unfortunate Events, A Lemony Snicket HarperCollins		Vocabulary/Literary Language/ Word meanings Writing Traits/Word choice
Seven Blind Mice Ed Young Philomel		Comprehension/Draw and support conclusions Structural Elements/Illustration
Shiloh Phyllis Reynolds Naylor Atheneum		Comprehension/Infer
Shrek! William Steig Farrar		Vocabulary/Literary Language/Alliteration Literary Elements and Devices/Hyperbole/ Obvious exaggeration
Sign of the Beaver Elizabeth George Speare Houghton Mifflin		Comprehension/Form literal and interpretive questions Literary Elements and Devices/Foreshadowing
Sky Dogs Jane Yolen Harcourt		Vocabulary/Literary Language/Onomatopoeia
Sleeping Ugly Jane Yolen Putnam		Literary Elements and Devices/Allusion
Smoky Night Eve Bunting Harcourt	Comprehension/Draw and support conclusions	Comprehension/Infer Comprehension/Determine importance Structural Elements/Illustration

Snowflake Bentley
Jacqueline Briggs Martin
Houghton Mifflin
	Comprehension/Determine importance
	Structural Elements/Character development
		Comprehension/Interpret
		Comprehension/Construct sensory images
		Comprehension/Identify main ideas
		Comprehension/Summarize
		Vocabulary/Literary Language/Literary/
		  Figurative language
		Vocabulary/Literary Language/Simile/
		  Metaphor
		Genre/Biography

	TITLE LIST	
Book Title, Author, and Publisher	**Mentor Lessons** **Strand/Standard**	**Booklinks** **Strand/Standard**
So Far from the Sea Eve Bunting Clarion	Literary Elements and Devices/Point of view	Comprehension/Connect to the culture/ experiences of others Comprehension/Summarize Structural Elements/Setting Structural Elements/Theme
So You Want to Be President? Judith St. George Philomel	Comprehension/Identify main ideas	Comprehension/Analyze critically Comprehension/Infer Comprehension/Compare/Contrast Structural Elements/Tone/Mood Genre/Distinguishing features of nonfiction
St. George and the Dragon Margaret Hodges Little, Brown		Structural Elements/Plot Vocabulary/Literary Language/Literary/ Figurative language
Stinky Cheese Man and Other Fairly Stupid Tales, ***The*** Jon Scieszka Viking		Literary Elements and Devices/Allusion
Stone Fox John Reynolds Gardiner HarperCollins		Comprehension/Make connections Vocabulary/Literary Language/Transition words
Story of Jumping Mouse, The John Steptoe HarperTrophy		Genre/Fairy tale/Folktale/Tall tale
Stranger, The Chris Van Allsburg Houghton Mifflin		Genre/Distinguishing features of fiction Genre/Fantasy
Summer of the Swans Betsy Byars Viking		Comprehension/Identify main ideas
Sweet Clara and the Freedom Quilt Deborah Hopkinson Scholastic		Comprehension/Represent text with an organizer Structural Elements/Plot Structural Elements/Dialogue Genre/Historical fiction
Sweetest Fig, The Chris Van Allsburg Houghton Mifflin		Literary Elements and Devices/Poetic justice Literary Elements and Devices/Irony
Sylvester and the Magic Pebble William Steig Windmill Books		Vocabulary/Literary Language/ Word meanings Literary Elements and Devices/Imagery

Book Title, Author, and Publisher	Mentor Lessons Strand/Standard	Booklinks Strand/Standard
Table Where Rich People Sit, The Byrd Baylor Aladdin		Comprehension/Analyze critically Structural Elements/Theme Literary Elements and Devices/Foreshadowing Literary Elements and Devices/Irony
Tale of Despereaux, The Kate DiCamillo Candlewick		Comprehension/Construct sensory images Literary Elements and Devices/Personification Genre/Fairy tale/Folktale/Tall tale
Tales of a Fourth Grade Nothing Judy Blume Puffin		Structural Elements/Character development
Tar Beach Faith Ringgold Crown Books	Vocabulary/Literary Language/Simile/ Metaphor	Literary Elements and Devices/Allusion Literary Elements and Devices/Symbolism
Thank You, Mr. Falker Patricia Polacco Philomel		Comprehension/Make connections Structural Elements/Climax Structural Elements/Tone/Mood
Three Little Wolves and the Big Bad Pig Eugene Trivizas Margaret K. McElderry		Literary Elements and Devices/Allusion
Three Pigs, The David Wiesner Clarion		Vocabulary/Literary Language/Onomatopoeia Genre/Fantasy
Through My Eyes Ruby Bridges Scholastic		Genre/Biography (autobiography)
Tough Cookie David Wisniewski HarperCollins	Literary Elements and Devices/Allusion	Structural Elements/Dialogue Vocabulary/Literary Language/Simile/ Metaphor Literary Elements and Devices/Point of view Literary Elements and Devices/Personification
Train to Somewhere, The Eve Bunting Clarion		Comprehension/Make connections
True Story of the Three Little Pigs, The Jon Scieszka Viking	Comprehension/Identify cause and effect Structural Elements/Dialogue	Structural Elements/Tone/Mood Vocabulary/Literary Language/ Word meanings Literary Elements and Devices/Point of view Literary Elements and Devices/Personification

Book Title, Author, and Publisher	Mentor Lessons Strand/Standard	Booklinks Strand/Standard
Tuck Everlasting Natalie Babbitt Farrar, Straus & Giroux		Structural Elements/Theme Vocabulary/Literary Language/Precise vocabulary Vocabulary/Literary Language/Literary/Figurative language
Tuesday David Wiesner Clarion	Genre/Fantasy	Structural Elements/Illustration
Two Bad Ants Chris Van Allsburg Houghton Mifflin	Comprehension/Activate and apply prior knowledge Structural Elements/Setting	Comprehension/Infer Structural Elements/Problem/Solution structure Literary Elements and Devices/Point of view
Ugly Duckling, The Jerry Pinkney Morrow		Genre/Fairy tale/Folktale/Tall tale
Under the Quilt of Night Deborah Hopkinson Atheneum/Anne Schwartz Books	Writing Traits/Voice	Vocabulary/Literary Language/Precise vocabulary Genre/Historical fiction Genre/Poetry Writing Traits/Word choice
Van Gogh Café, The Cynthia Rylant Harcourt		Comprehension/Infer
View from Saturday, The E. L. Konigsburg Atheneum		Vocabulary/Literary Language/Precise vocabulary
Wall, The Eve Bunting Clarion		Comprehension/Activate and apply prior knowledge Comprehension/Determine purpose
Wayside School Is Falling Down Louis Sachar HarperCollins		Structural Elements/Tone/Mood
Westing Game, The Ellen Raskin Dutton Juvenile		Genre/Distinguishing features of fiction
When I Was Young in the Mountains Cynthia Rylant Dutton	Structural Elements/Main idea	Structural Elements/Setting Vocabulary/Literary Language/Repetition

Book Title, Author, and Publisher	Mentor Lessons Strand/Standard	Booklinks Strand/Standard
Where the Red Fern Grows Wilson Rawls Delacorte		Structural Elements/Problem/ Solution structure
Where the Sidewalk Ends Shel Silverstein HarperCollins		Vocabulary/Literary Language/ Transition words Genre/Poetry
Whipping Boy, The Sid Fleischman Greenwillow		Comprehension/Represent text with an organizer
Why Mosquitoes Buzz in People's Ears Verna Aardema Puffin		Literary Elements and Devices/Poetic justice
Widow's Broom, The Chris Van Allsburg Scholastic	Literary Elements and Devices/Poetic justice	
Wilma Unlimited Kathleen Krull Harcourt	Vocabulary/Literary Language/Transition words	Comprehension/Form literal and interpretive questions Structural Elements/Problem/Solution structure Structural Elements/Main idea Genre/Biography Writing Traits/Organization
Wreck of the Zephyr, The Chris Van Allsburg Houghton Mifflin	Literary Elements and Devices/Flashback	
Wrinkle in Time, A Madeleine L'Engle Farrar, Straus & Giroux		Comprehension/Summarize
Yellow Star, The Carmen Agra Deedy Peachtree	Comprehension/Analyze critically Literary Elements and Devices/Foreshadowing	Comprehension/Activate and apply prior knowledge Structural Elements/Climax Literary Elements and Devices/Irony
Yo! Yes? Richard Jackson Orchard		Writing Traits/Conventions
Yo, Hungry Wolf! David Vozar Doubleday		Structural Elements/Tone/Mood
Z Was Zapped, The Chris Van Allsburg Houghton Mifflin	Vocabulary/Literary Language/Alliteration Writing Traits/Organization	

CALDECOTT AWARD WINNERS

Book Title	Author	Publisher	Year Published	Caldecott Date
Flotsam	David Wiesner	Clarion	2006	2007
Gone Wild	David McLimans	Walker	2006	2007
Moses: When Harriet Tubman Led Her People to Freedom	Carole Boston Weatherford	Hyperion	2006	2007
Hot-Air: The (Mostly) True Story of the First Hot Air Balloon Ride	Marjorie Priceman	Atheneum	2005	2006
Rosa	Nikki Giovanni	Henry Holt	2005	2006
Song of the Water Boatman and Other Pond Poems	Joyce Sidman	Houghton Mifflin	2005	2006
The Hello, Goodbye Window	Norton Juster	Hyperion	2005	2006
Zen Shorts	Jon J. Muth	Scholastic	2005	2006
Kitten's First Full Moon	Kevin Henkes	Greenwillow	2005	2005
Coming on Home Soon	Jacqueline Woodson	GP Putnam/ Penguin	2004	2005
Knuffle Bunny: A Cautionary Tale	Mo Willems	Hyperion	2004	2005
The Red Book	Barbara Lehman	Houghton Mifflin	2004	2005
Don't Let the Pigeon Drive the Bus!	Mo Willems	Hyperion	2003	2004
Ella Sarah Gets Dressed	Margaret Chodos-Irvine	Harcourt	2003	2004
The Man Who Walked Between the Towers	Mordicai Gerstein	Roaring Brook Press	2003	2004
What Do You Do with a Tail Like This?	Steve Jenkins/Robin Page	Houghton Mifflin	2003	2004
Hondo and Fabian	Peter McCarty	Henry Holt	2002	2003
My Friend Rabbit	Eric Rohmann	Roaring Brook	2002	2003
Noah's Ark	Jerry Pinkney	SeaStar Books	2002	2003
The Spider and the Fly	Tony DiTerlizzi	Simon & Schuster	2002	2003
Martin's Big Words: The Life of Dr. Martin Luther King, Jr.	Doreen Rappaport	Hyperion	2001	2002
The Dinosaurs of Waterhouse Hawkins	Barbara Kerley	Scholastic	2001	2002
The Stray Dog	Marc Simont	HarperCollins	2001	2002
The Three Pigs	David Wiesner	Houghton Mifflin	2001	2002
Casey at the Bat	Ernest Thayer	Handprint	2000	2001
Click, Clack, Moo: Cows That Type	Doreen Cronin	Simon & Schuster	2000	2001
Olivia	Ian Falconer	Atheneum	2000	2001
So You Want to Be President?	Judith St. George	Philomel	2000	2001
A Child's Calendar	John Updike	Holiday House	1999	2000
Joseph Had a Little Overcoat	Simms Taback	Viking	1999	2000

CALDECOTT AWARD WINNERS

Book Title	Author	Publisher	Year Published	Caldecott Date
Sector 7	David Wiesner	Clarion	1999	2000
The Ugly Duckling	Jerry Pinkney	Morrow	1999	2000
When Sophie Gets Angry—Really, Really Angry...	Molly Bang	Scholastic	1999	2000
Duke Ellington: The Piano Prince and the Orchestra	Andrea Davis Pinkney	Hyperion	1998	1999
No, David!	David Shannon	Scholastic	1998	1999
Snow	Uri Shulevitz	Farrar	1998	1999
Snowflake Bentley	Jacqueline Briggs Martin	Houghton Mifflin	1998	1999
Tibet Through the Red Box	Peter Sis	Frances Foster	1998	1999
Harlem	Walter Dean Myers	Scholastic	1997	1998
Rapunzel	Paul O. Zelinsky	Dutton	1997	1998
The Gardener	Sarah Stewart	Farrar	1997	1998
There Was an Old Lady Who Swallowed a Fly	Simms Taback	Viking	1997	1998
Golem	David Wisniewski	Clarion	1996	1997
Hush! A Thai Lullaby	Minfong Ho	Orchard	1996	1997
Starry Messenger	Peter Sis	Frances Foster/ Farrar	1996	1997
The Graphic Alphabet	David Pelletier	Orchard	1996	1997
The Paperboy	Dav Pilkey	Orchard	1996	1997
Alphabet City	Stephen Johnson	Viking	1995	1996
Officer Buckle and Gloria	Peggy Rathmann	Putnam	1995	1996
Some Smug Slug	Pamela Duncan Edwards	Harper Trophy	1995	1996
The Faithful Friend	Robert D. San Souci	Simon & Schuster	1995	1996
Tops & Bottoms	Janet Stevens	Harcourt	1995	1996
Zin! Zin! Zin! A Violin	Lloyd Moss	Simon & Schuster	1995	1996
John Henry	Julius Lester	Dial	1994	1995
Smoky Night	Eve Bunting	Harcourt	1994	1995
Swamp Angel	Anne Issacs	Dutton	1994	1995
Time Flies	Eric Rohmann	Crown	1994	1995
Grandfather's Journey	Allen Say	Houghton Mifflin	1993	1994
In the Small, Small Pond	Denise Fleming	Holt	1993	1994
Owen	Kevin Henkes	Greenwillow	1993	1994
Peppe the Lamplighter	Elisa Bartone	Lothrop	1993	1994
Raven: A Trickster Tale from the Pacific Northwest	Gerald McDermott	Harcourt	1993	1994

CALDECOTT AWARD WINNERS

Book Title	Author	Publisher	Year Published	Caldecott Date
Yo! Yes?	Richard Jackson	Orchard	1993	1994
Mirette on the High Wire	Emily Arnold McCully	Putnam	1992	1993
Seven Blind Mice	Ed Young	Philomel	1992	1993
The Stinky Cheese Man and Other Fairly Stupid Tales	Jon Scieszka	Viking	1992	1993
Working Cotton	Sherley Anne Williams	Harcourt	1992	1993
Tar Beach	Faith Ringgold	Crown Publishers	1991	1992
Tuesday	David Wiesner	Clarion	1991	1992
Black and White	David Macaulay	Houghton Mifflin	1990	1991
"More More More," Said the Baby	Vera B. Williams	Greenwillow	1990	1991
Puss in Boots	Malcolm Arthur	Di Capua/Farrar	1990	1991
Bill Peet: An Autobiography	Bill Peet	Houghton Mifflin	1989	1990
Color Zoo	Lois Ehlert	Lippincott	1989	1990
Hershel and the Hanukkah Goblins	Eric Kimmel	Holiday House	1989	1990
Lon Po Po: A Red-Riding Hood Story from China	Ed Young	Philomel	1989	1990
The Talking Eggs: A Folktale from the American South	Robert D. San Souci	Dial	1989	1990
Free Fall	David Wiesner	Lothrop	1988	1989
Goldilocks and the Three Bears	James Marshall	Dial	1988	1989
Mirandy and Brother Wind	Patricia C. McKissack	Knopf	1988	1989
Song and Dance Man	Karen Ackerman	Knopf	1988	1989
The Boy of the Three-Year Nap	Diane Snyder	Houghton Mifflin	1988	1989
Mufaro's Beautiful Daughters: An African Tale	John Steptoe	Lothrop	1987	1988
Owl Moon	Jane Yolen	Philomel	1987	1988
Alphabatics	Suse MacDonald	Bradbury	1986	1987
Hey, Al	Arthur Yorinks	Farrar	1986	1987
Rumpelstiltskin	Paul O. Zelinsky	Dutton	1986	1987
The Village of Round and Square Houses	Ann Grifalconi	Little, Brown	1986	1987
King Bidgood's in the Bathtub	Audrey Wood	Harcourt	1985	1986
The Polar Express	Chris Van Allsburg	Houghton Mifflin	1985	1986
The Relatives Came	Cynthia Rylant	Bradbury	1985	1986
Hansel and Gretel	Rika Lesser	Dodd	1984	1985
Have You Seen My Duckling?	Nancy Tafuri	Greenwillow	1984	1985
Saint George and the Dragon	Margaret Hodges	Little, Brown	1984	1985

CALDECOTT AWARD WINNERS

Book Title	Author	Publisher	Year Published	Caldecott Date
The Story of Jumping Mouse: A Native American Legend	John Steptoe	Lothrop	1984	1985
Little Red Riding Hood	Trina Schart Hyman	Holiday	1983	1984
Ten, Nine, Eight	Molly Bang	Greenwillow	1983	1984
The Glorious Flight: Across the Channel with Louis Bleriot	Alice & Martin Provensen	Viking	1983	1984
A Chair for My Mother	Vera B. Williams	Greenwillow	1982	1983
Shadow	Marcia Brown	Scribner	1982	1983
When I Was Young in the Mountains	Cynthia Rylant	Dutton	1982	1983
A Visit to William Blake's Inn: Poems for Innocent and Experienced Travelers	Nancy Willard	Harcourt	1981	1982
Jumanji	Chris Van Allsburg	Houghton Mifflin	1981	1982
On Market Street	Arnold Lobel	Grenwillow	1981	1982
Outside Over There	Maurice Sendak	Harper	1981	1982
Where the Buffaloes Begin	Olaf Baker	Warne	1981	1982
Fables	Arnold Lobel	Harper	1980	1981
Mice Twice	Joseph Low	Atheneum	1980	1981
The Bremen-Town Musicians	Ilse Plume	Doubleday	1980	1981
The Gray Lady and the Strawberry Snatcher	Molly Bang	Four Winds	1980	1981
Truck	Donald Crews	Grenwillow	1980	1981
Ben's Trumpet	Rachel Isadora	Greenwillow	1979	1980
Ox-cart Man	Donald Hall	Viking	1979	1980
The Garden of Abdul Gasazi	Chris Van Allsburg	Houghton Mifflin	1979	1980
The Treasure	Uri Shulevitz	Farrar	1979	1980
Freight Train	Donald Crews	Greenwillow	1978	1979
The Girl Who Loved Wild Horses	Paul Goble	Bradbury	1978	1979
The Way to Start a Day	Byrd Baylor	Scribner	1978	1979
Castle	David Macaulay	Houghton Mifflin	1977	1978
It Could Always Be Worse	Margot Zemach	Farrar	1977	1978
Noah's Ark	Peter Spier	Doubleday	1977	1978
Ashanti to Zulu: African Traditions	Margaret Musgrove	Dial	1976	1977
Fish for Supper	M. B. Goffstein	Dial	1976	1977
Hawk, I'm Your Brother	Byrd Baylor	Scribner	1976	1977
The Amazing Bone	William Steig	Farrar	1976	1977
The Contest	Nonny Hogrogian	Greenwillow	1976	1977
The Golem: A Jewish Legend	Beverly Brodsky McKermott	Lippincott	1976	1977

CALDECOTT AWARD WINNERS

Book Title	Author	Publisher	Year Published	Caldecott Date
Strega Nona	Tomie dePaola	Prentice-Hall	1975	1976
The Desert Is Theirs	Byrd Baylor	Scribner	1975	1976
Why Mosquitoes Buzz in People's Ears: A West African Tale	Verna Aardema	Dial	1975	1976
Arrow to the Sun	Gerald McDermott	Biking	1974	1975
Jambo Means Hello: Swahili Alphabet Book	Muriel Feelings	Dial	1974	1975
Cathedral	David Macaulay	Houghton Mifflin	1973	1974
Duffy and The Devil	Harve Zemach	Farrar	1973	1974
Three Jovial Huntsmen	Susan Jeffers	Bradbury	1973	1974
Anansi the Spider: A Tale from the Ashanti	Gerald McDermott	Holt	1972	1973
Hosie's Alphabet	Hosea Tobias and Lisa Baskin	Viking	1972	1973
Snow-White and the Seven Dwarfs	Randall Jarrell	Farrar	1972	1973
The Funny Little Woman	Arlene Mosel	Dutton	1972	1973
When Clay Sings	Byrd Baylor	Scribner	1972	1973
Hildilid's Night	Cheli Duran Ryan	Macmillan	1971	1972
If All the Seas Were One Sea	Janina Domanska	Macmillan	1971	1972
Moja Means One: Swahili Counting Book	Muriel Feelings	Dial	1971	1972
One Fine Day	Nonny Hogrogian	Macmillan	1971	1972
A Story, A Story	Gail E. Haley	Atheneum	1970	1971
Frog and Toad Are Friends	Arnold Lobel	HarperCollins	1970	1971
In the Night Kitchen	Maurice Sendak	Harper	1970	1971
The Angry Moon	William Sleator	Atlantic	1970	1971
Alexander and the Wind-Up Mouse	Leo Lionni	Pantheon	1969	1970
Goggles!	Ezra Jack Keats	Macmillan	1969	1970
Pop Corn and Ma Goodness	Edna Mitchell Preston	Viking	1969	1970
Sylvester and the Magic Pebble	William Steig	Windmill Books	1969	1970
The Judge: An Untrue Tale	Harve Zemach	Farrar	1969	1970
Thy Friend, Obadiah	Brinton Turkle	Viking	1969	1970
The Fool of the World and the Flying Ship	Arthur Ransome	Farrar	1968	1969
Why the Sun and the Moon Live in the Sky	Elphinstone Dayrell	Houghton Mifflin	1968	1969
Drummer Hoff	Barbara Emberley	Prentice-Hall	1967	1968
Frederick	Leo Lionni	Pantheon	1967	1968
Seashore Story	Taro Yashima	Viking	1967	1968

CALDECOTT AWARD WINNERS

Book Title	Author	Publisher	Year Published	Caldecott Date
The Emperor and the Kite	Jane Yolen	World	1967	1968
One Wide River to Cross	Barbara Emberley	Prentice-Hall	1966	1967
Sam, Bangs & Moonshine	Evaline Ness	Holt	1966	1967
Always Room for One More	Leclair Alger	Holt	1965	1966
Hide and Seek Fog	Alvin Tresselt	Lothrop	1965	1966
Just Me	Marie Hall Ets	Viking	1965	1966
Tom Tit Tot	Evaline Ness	Scribner	1965	1966
A Pocketful of Cricket	Rebecca Caudill	Holt	1964	1965
May I Bring a Friend?	Beatrice Schenk de Regniers	Atheneum	1964	1965
Rain Makes Applesauce	Julian Scheer	Holiday	1964	1965
The Wave	Margaret Hodges	Houghton Mifflin	1964	1965
All in the Morning Early	Leclair Alger	Holt	1963	1964
Mother Goose and Nursery Rhymes	Philip Reed	Atheneum	1963	1964
Swimmy	Leo Lionni	Pantheon	1963	1964
Where the Wild Things Are	Maurice Sendak	Harper	1963	1964
Mr. Rabbit and the Lovely Present	Charlotte Zolotow	Harper	1962	1963
The Snowy Day	Ezra Jack Keats	Viking	1962	1963
The Sun Is a Golden Earring	Natalia M. Belting	Holt	1962	1963
Fox Went Out on a Chilly Night: An Old Song	Peter Spier	Doubleday	1961	1962
Little Bear's Visit	Else H. Minarik	Harper	1961	1962
Once a Mouse	Marcia Brown	Scribner	1961	1962
The Day We Saw the Sun Come Up	Alice Goudey	Scribner	1961	1962
Baboushka and the Three Kings	Ruth Robbins	Parnassus	1960	1961
Inch by Inch	Leo Lionni	Obolensky	1960	1961
Houses from the Sea	Alice E. Goudey	Scribner	1959	1960
Nine Days to Christmas	Marie Hall Ets and Aurora Labastida	Viking	1959	1960
The Moon Jumpers	Janice May Udry	Harper	1959	1960
Chanticleer and the Fox	Barbara Cooney	Crowell	1958	1959
The House That Jack Built: La Maison Qu Jacques a Batie	Antonio Frasconi	Harcourt	1958	1959
Umbrella	Taro Yashima	Viking	1958	1959
What Do You Say, Dear?	Sesyle Joslin	W.R. Scott	1958	1959
Anatole and the Cat	Eve Titus	McGraw-Hill	1957	1958
Fly High, Fly Low	Don Freeman	Viking	1957	1958

CALDECOTT AWARD WINNERS

Book Title	Author	Publisher	Year Published	Caldecott Date
Time of Wonder	Robert McCloskey	Viking	1957	1958
1 Is One	Tasha Tudor	Walck	1956	1957
A Tree Is Nice	Janice Udry	Harper	1956	1957
Anatole	Eve Titus	McGraw-Hill	1956	1957
Gillespie and the Guards	Benjamin Elkin	Viking	1956	1957
Lion	William Pene du Bois	Viking	1956	1957
Mr. Penny's Race Horse	Marie Hall Ets	Viking	1956	1957
Crow Boy	Taro Yashima	Viking	1955	1956
Frog Went A-Courtin'	John Langstaff	Harcourt	1955	1956
Play With Me	Marie Hall Ets	Viking	1955	1956
Book of Nursery and Mother Goose Rhymes	Marguerite de Angeli	Doubleday	1954	1955
Cinderella, or the Little Glass Slipper	Marcia Brown	Scribner	1954	1955
The Thanksgiving Story	Alice Dalgliesh	Scribner	1954	1955
Wheel on the Chimney	Margaret Wise Brown	Lippincott	1954	1955
A Very Special House	Ruth Krauss	Harper	1953	1954
Green Eyes	A. Birnbaum	Capitol	1953	1954
Journey Cake, Ho!	Ruth Sawyer	Viking	1953	1954
Madeline's Rescue	Ludwig Bemelmans	Viking	1953	1954
The Steadfast Tin Soldier	Hans Christian Anderson	Scribner	1953	1954
When Will the World Be Mine?	Miriam Schlein	W.R. Scott	1953	1954
Ape in a Cape: An Alphabet of Odd Animals	Fritz Eichenberg	Harcourt	1952	1953
Five Little Monkeys	Juliet Kepes	Houghton Mifflin	1952	1953
One Morning in Maine	Robert McCloskey	Viking	1952	1953
Puss in Boots	Marcia Brown	Scribner	1952	1953
The Biggest Bear	Lynd Ward	Houghton Mifflin	1952	1953
The Storm Book	Charlotte Zolotow	Harper	1952	1953
All Falling Down	Gene Zion	Harper	1951	1952
Bear Party	William Pene du Bois	Viking	1951	1952
Feather Mountain	Elizabeth Olds	Houghton Mifflin	1951	1952
Finders Keepers	William Lipkind	Harcourt	1951	1952
Mr. T. W. Anthony Woo	Marie Hall Ets	Viking	1951	1952
Skipper John's Cook	Marcia Brown	Scribner	1951	1952
Dick Whittington and His Cat	Marcia Brown	Scribner	1950	1951
If I Ran the Zoo	Dr. Seuss	Random House	1950	1951

CALDECOTT AWARD WINNERS

Book Title	Author	Publisher	Year Published	Caldecott Date
T-Bone, the Baby Sitter	Clare Turlay Newberry	Harper	1950	1951
The Egg Tree	Katherine Milhous	Scribner	1950	1951
The Most Wonderful Doll in the World	Phyllis McGinley	Lippincott	1950	1951
The Two Reds	Nicolas Mordvinoff	Harcourt	1950	1951
America's Ethan Allen	Stewart Holbrook	Houghton Mifflin	1949	1950
Bartholomew and the Oobleck	Dr. Seuss	Random House	1949	1950
Henry Fisherman	Marcia Brown	Atheneum	1949	1950
Song of the Swallows	Leo Politi	Scribner	1949	1950
The Happy Day	Ruth Krauss	Harper	1949	1950
The Wild Birthday Cake	Lavinia R. Davis	Doubleday	1949	1950
All Around the Town	Phyllis McGinley	Lippincott	1948	1949
Blueberries for Sal	Robert McCloskey	Viking	1948	1949
Fish in the Air	Kurt Wiese	Viking	1948	1949
Juanita	Leo Politi	Scribner	1948	1949
The Big Snow	Berta and Elmer Hader	Macmillan	1948	1949
Bambino the Clown	Georges Schreiber	Viking	1947	1948
McElligot's Pool	Dr. Seuss	Random House	1947	1948
Roger and the Fox	Lavinia R. Davis	Doubleday	1947	1948
Song of Robin Hood	Anne Malcolmson	Houghton Mifflin	1947	1948
Stone Soup	Marcia Brown	Scribner	1947	1948
The Important Book	Margaret Wise Brown	Harper Row	1947	1948
White Snow, Bright Snow	Alvin Tresselt	Lothrop	1947	1948
Boats on the River	Marjorie Flack	Viking	1946	1947
Pedro, the Angel of Olvera Street	Leo Politi	Scribner	1946	1947
Rain Drop Splash	Alvin Tresselt	Lothrop	1946	1947
Sing in Praise: A Collection of the Best Loved Hymns	Opal Wheeler	Dutton	1946	1947
The Little Island	Margaret Wise Brown	Doubleday	1946	1947
Timothy Turtle	Al Graham	Welch	1946	1947
Little Lost Lamb	Margaret Wise Brown	Doubleday	1945	1946
My Mother Is the Most Beautiful Woman in the World	Becky Reyher	Lothrop	1945	1946
Sing Mother Goose	Opal Wheeler	Dutton	1945	1946
The Rooster Crows	Maude and Miska Petersham	Macmillan	1945	1946

CALDECOTT AWARD WINNERS

Book Title	Author	Publisher	Year Published	Caldecott Date
You Can Write Chinese	Kurt Wiese	Viking	1945	1946
In the Forest	Marie Hall Ets	Viking	1944	1945
Mother Goose	Tasha Tudor	Oxford Press	1944	1945
Prayer for a Child	Rachel Field	Macmillan	1944	1945
The Christmas Anna Angel	Ruth Sawyer	Viking	1944	1945
Yonie Wondernose	Marguerite de Angeli	Doubleday	1944	1945
A Child's Good Night Book	Margaret Wise Brown	W.R. Scott	1943	1944
Good Luck Horse	Chih-Yi Chan	Whittlesey	1943	1944
Many Moons	James Thurber	Harcourt	1943	1944
Pierre Pidgeon	Lee Kingman	Houghton Mifflin	1943	1944
Small Rain: Verses from the Bible	Jessie Orton Jones	Viking	1943	1944
The Mighty Hunter	Berta and Elmer Hader	Macmillan	1943	1944
Dash and Dart	Mary and Conrad Buff	Viking	1942	1943
Marshmallow	Clare Turlay Newberry	Harper	1942	1943
The Little House	Virginia Lee Burton	Houghton Mifflin	1942	1943
An American ABC	Maude and Miska Petersham	Macmillan	1941	1942
In My Mother's House	Ann Nolan Clark	Viking	1941	1942
Make Way for Ducklings	Robert McCloskey	Viking	1941	1942
Nothing at All	Wanda Gag	Coward	1941	1942
Paddle-to-the-Sea	Holling C. Holling	Houghton Mifflin	1941	1942
April's Kittens	Clare Turlay Newberry	Harper	1940	1941
They Were Strong and Good	Robert Lawson	Viking	1940	1941
Abraham Lincoln	Ingri and Edgar Parin d'Aulaire	Doubleday	1939	1940
Cock-a-Doodle Doo	Berta and Elmer Hader	Macmillan	1939	1940
Madeline	Ludwig Bemelmans	Viking	1939	1940
The Ageless Story	Lauren Ford	Dodd	1939	1940
Andy and the Lion	James Daugherty	Viking	1938	1939
Barkis	Clare Turlay Newberry	Harper	1938	1939
Mei Li	Thomas Handforth	Doubleday	1938	1939
Snow White and the Seven Dwarfs	Wanda Gag	Coward	1938	1939
The Forest Pool	Laura Adams Armer	Longmans	1938	1939
Wee Gillis	Munro Leaf	Viking	1938	1939
Animals of the Bible	Helen Dean Fish	Lippincott	1937	1938
Four and Twenty Blackbirds	Helen Dean Fish	Stokes	1937	1938
Seven Simeons: A Russian Tale	Boris Artzybasheff	Viking	1937	1938

Newbery Medal

The Newbery Medal was named for eighteenth-century British bookseller John Newbery. It is awarded annually by the Association for Library Service to Children, a division of the American Library Association, to the author of the most distinguished contribution to American literature for children.

NEWBERY AWARD WINNERS			
Book Title	Author	Publisher	Year Published
The Higher Power of Lucky	Susan Patron	Simon & Schuster	2007
Penny from Heaven	Jennifer L. Holm	Random House	2007
Hattie Big Sky	Kirby Larson	Delacorte Press	2007
Rules	Cynthia Lord	Scholastic	2007
Criss Cross	Lynne Rae Perkins	Greenwillow Books	2006
Whittington	Alan Armstrong	Random House	2006
Hitler Youth: Growing Up in Hitler's Shadow	Susan Campbell Bartoletti	Scholastic	2006
Princess Academy	Shannon Hale	Bloomsbury Children's Books	2006
Show Way	Jacqueline Woodson	G.P. Putnam's Sons	2006
Kira-Kira	Cynthia Kadohata	Atheneum	2005
Al Capone Does My Shirts	Gennifer Choldenko	G.P. Putnam's Sons	2005
The Voice That Challenged a Nation: Marian Anderson and the Struggle for Equal Rights	Russell Freedman	Clarion Books/ Houghton Mifflin	2005
Lizzie Bright and the Buckminster Boy	Gary D. Schmidt	Clarion Books/ Houghton Mifflin	2005
The Tale of Despereaux: Being the Story of a Mouse, A Princess, Some Soup, and a Spool of Thread	Kate DeCamillo	Candlewick Press	2004
Olive's Ocean	Kevin Henkes	Greenwillow Books	2004
An American Plague: The True and Terrifying Story of the Yellow Fever Epidemic of 1793	Jim Murphy	Clarion Books	2004
Crispin: The Cross of Lead	Avi	Hyperion Books	2003
The House of the Scorpion	Nancy Farmer	Atheneum	2003
Pictures of Hollis Woods	Patricia Reilly Giff	Random House/ Wendy Lamb Books	2003
Hoot	Carl Hiaasen	Knopf	2003
A Corner of the Universe	Ann M. Martin	Scholastic	2003
Surviving the Applewhites	Stephanie S. Tolan	HarperCollins	2003
A Single Shard	Linda Sue Park	Houghton Mifflin/Clarion	2002
Everything on a Waffle	Polly Horvath	Farrar, Straus & Giroux	2002

NEWBERY AWARD WINNERS

Book Title	Author	Publisher	Year Published
Carver: A Life in Poems	Marilyn Nelson	Front Street	2002
A Year Down Yonder	Richard Peck	Dial	2001
Hope Was Here	Joan Bauer	G.P. Putnam's Sons	2001
Because of Winn-Dixie	Kate DiCamillo	Candlewick Press	2001
Joey Pigza Loses Control	Jack Gantos	Farrar, Straus & Giroux	2001
The Wanderer	Sharon Creech	Joanna Cotler Books/ HarperCollins	2001
Bud, Not Buddy	Christopher Paul Curtis	Delacorte	2000
Getting Near to Baby	Audrey Couloumbis	Putnam	2000
Our Only May Amelia	Jennifer L. Holm	HarperCollins	2000
26 Fairmount Avenue	Tomie dePaola	Putnam	2000
Holes	Louis Sachar	Frances Foster	1999
A Long Way from Chicago	Richard Peck	Dial	1999
Out of the Dust	Karen Hesse	Scholastic	1998
Ella Enchanted	Gail Carson Levine	HarperCollins	1998
Lily's Crossing	Patricia Reilly Giff	Delacorte	1998
Wringer	Jerry Spinelli	HarperCollins	1998
The View from Saturday	E.L. Konigsburg	Jean Karl/Atheneum	1997
A Girl Named Disaster	Nancy Farmer	Richard Jackson/ Orchard Books	1997
Moorchild	Eloise McGraw	Margaret McElderry/ Simon & Schuster	1997
The Thief	Megan Whalen Turner	Greenwillow/Morrow	1997
Belle Prater's Boy	Ruth White	Farrar, Straus & Giroux	1997
The Midwide's Apprentice	Karen Cushman	Clarion	1996
What Jamie Saw	Carolyn Coman	Front Street	1996
The Watsons Go to Birmingham: 1963	Christopher Paul Curtis	Delacorte	1996
Yolonda's Genius	Carol Fenner	Margaret K. McElderry/ Simon & Schuster	1996
The Great Fire	Jim Murphy	Scholastic	1996
Walk Two Moons	Sharon Creech	HarperCollins	1995
Catherine, Called Birdy	Karen Cushman	Clarion	1995
The Ear, the Eye and the Arm	Nancy Farmer	Jackson/Orchard	1995
The Giver	Lois Lowry	Houghton Mifflin	1994
Crazy Lady	Jane Leslie Conly	HarperCollins	1994
Dragon's Gate	Laurence Yep	HarperCollins	1994

NEWBERY AWARD WINNERS

Book Title	Author	Publisher	Year Published
Eleanor Roosevelt: A Life of Discovery	Russell Freedman	Clarion Books	1994
Missing May	Cynthia Rylant	Jackson/Orchard	1993
What Hearts	Bruce Brooks	A Laura Geringer Book, a HarperCollins imprint	1993
The Dark-Thirty: Southern Tales of the Supernatural	Patricia McKissack	Knopf	1993
Somewhere in the Darkness	Walter Dean Myers	Scholastic Hardcover	1993
Shiloh	Phyllis Reynolds Naylor	Atheneum	1992
Nothing But the Truth: A Documentary Novel	Avi	Jackson/Orchard	1992
The Wright Brothers: How They Invented the Airplane	Russell Freedman	Holiday House	1992
Maniac McGee	Jerry Spinelli	Little, Brown	1991
The True Confessions of Charlotte Doyle	Avi	Jackson/Orchard	1991
Number the Stars	Lois Lowry	Houghton Mifflin	1990
Afternoon of the Elves	Janet Taylor Lisle	Jackson/Orchard	1990
Shabanu, Daughter of the Wind	Suzanne Fisher Staples	Knopf	1990
The Winter Room	Gary Paulsen	Jackson/Orchard	1990
Joyful Noise: Poems for Two Voices	Paul Fleischman	HarperCollins	1989
In the Beginning: Creation Stories from Around the World	Virginia Hamilton	Harcourt	1989
Scorpions	Walter Dean Myers	Harper	1989
Lincoln: A Photobiography	Russell Freeman	Clarion	1988
After the Rain	Norma Fox Mazer	Morrow	1988
Hatchet	Gary Paulsen	Bradbury	1988
The Whipping Boy	Sid Fleischman	Greenwillow	1987
A Fine White Dust	Cynthia Rylant	Bradbury	1987
On My Honor	Marion Dane Bauer	Clarion	1987
Volcano: The Eruption and Healing of Mount St. Helens	Patricia Lauber	Bradbury	1987
Sarah, Plain and Tall	Patricia MacLachlan	HarperCollins	1986
Commodore Perry in the Land of the Shogun	Rhoda Blumberg	Lothrop	1986
Dogsong	Gary Paulsen	Bradbury	1986
The Hero and the Crown	Robin McKinley	Greenwillow	1985
Like Jake and Me	Mavis Jukes	Knopf	1985
The Moves Make the Man	Bruce Brooks	Harper	1985
One-Eyed Cat	Paula Fox	Bradbury	1985
Dear Mr. Henshaw	Beverly Cleary	Morrow	1984
The Sign of the Beaver	Elizabeth George Speare	Houghton	1984

NEWBERY AWARD WINNERS

Book Title	Author	Publisher	Year Published
A Solitary Blue	Cynthia Voigt	Atheneum	1984
Sugaring Time	Kathryn Lasky	Macmillan	1984
The Wish Giver: Three Tales of Coven Tree	Bill Brittain	Harper	1984
Dicey's Song	Cynthia Voigt	Atheneum	1983
Doctor De Soto	William Steig	Farrar	1983
Graven Images	Paul Fleischman	Harper	1983
Homesick: My Own Story	Jean Fritz	Putnam	1983
Sweet Whispers, Brother Rush	Virginia Hamilton	Philomel	1983
A Visit to William Blake's Inn: Poems for Innocent and Experienced Travelers	Nancy Willard	Harcourt	1982
Ramona Quimby, Age 8	Beverly Cleary	Morrow	1982
Upon the Head of the Goat: A Childhood in Hungary 1939–1944	Aranka Siegal	Farrar	1982
The Fledgling	Jane Langton	Harper	1981
A Ring of Endless Light	Madeleine L'Engle	Farrar	1981
Jacob Have I Loved	Katherine Paterson	Crowell	1981
A Gathering of Days: A New England Girl's Journal, 1830–1832	Joan W. Blos	Scribner	1980
The Road from Home: The Story of an Armenian Girl	David Kherdian	Greenwillow	1980
The Westing Game	Ellen Raskin	Dutton	1979
The Great Gilly Hopkins	Katherine Paterson	Crowell	1979
Bridge to Terabithia	Katherine Paterson	Crowell	1978
Ramona and Her Father	Beverly Cleary	Morrow	1978
Anpao: An American Indian Odyssey	Jamake Highwater	Lippincott	1978
Roll of Thunder, Hear My Cry	Mildred D. Taylor	Dial	1977
Abel's Island	William Steig	Farrar	1977
A String in the Harp	Nancy Bond	Atheneum	1977
The Grey King	Susan Cooper	McElderry/Atheneum	1976
The Hundred Penny Box	Sharon Bell Mathis	Viking	1976
Dragonwings	Laurence Yep	Harper	1976
M. C. Higgins, the Great	Virginia Hamilton	Macmillan	1975
Figgs & Phantoms	Ellen Raskin	Dutton	1975
My Brother Sam Is Dead	James Lincoln Collier & Christopher Collier	Four Winds	1975
The Perilous Gard	Elizabeth Marie Pope	Houghton	1975
Philip Hall Likes Me, I Reckon Maybe	Bette Greene	Dial	1975

NEWBERY AWARD WINNERS

Book Title	Author	Publisher	Year Published
The Slave Dancer	Paula Fox	Bradbury	1974
The Dark Is Rising	Susan Cooper	McElderry/Atheneum	1974
Julie of the Wolves	Jean Craighead George	Harper	1973
Frog and Toad Together	Arnold Lobel	Harper	1973
The Upstairs Room	Johanna Reiss	Crowell	1973
The Witches of Worm	Zilpha Keatley Snyder	Atheneum	1973
Mrs. Frisby and the Rats of NIMH	Robert C. O'Brien	Atheneum	1972
Incident at Hawk's Hill	Allan W. Eckert	Little, Brown	1972
The Planet of Junior Brown	Virginia Hamilton	Macmillan	1972
The Tombs of Atuan	Ursula K. LeGuin	Atheneum	1972
Annie and the Old One	Miska Miles	Little, Brown	1972
The Headless Cupid	Zilpha Keatley Snyder	Atheneum	1972
Summer of the Swans	Betsy Byars	Viking	1971
Knee Knock Rise	Natalie Babbitt	Farrar	1971
Enchantress from the Stars	Sylvia Louise Engdahl	Atheneum	1971
Sing Down the Moon	Scott O'Dell	Houghton	1971
Sounder	William H. Armstrong	Harper	1970
Our Eddie	Sulamith Ish-Kishor	Pantheon	1970
The Many Ways of Seeing: An Introduction to the Pleasure of Art	Janet Gaylord Moore	World	1970
Journey Outside	Mary Q. Steele	Viking	1970
The High King	Lloyd Alexander	Holt	1969
To Be a Slave	Julius Lester	Dial	1969
When Shlemiel Went to Warsaw and Other Stories	Isaac Bashevis Singer	Farrar	1969
From the Mixed-Up Files of Mrs. Basil E. Frankweiler	E.L. Konigsburg	Atheneum	1968
Jennifer, Hecate, Macbeth, William McKinley, and Me, Elizabeth	E.L. Konigsburg	Atheneum	1968
The Black Pearl	Scott O'Dell	Houghton Mifflin	1968
The Fearsome Inn	Isaac Bashevis Singer	Scribner's	1968
The Eqypt Game	Zilpha Keatley Snyder	Atheneum	1968
Up a Road Slowly	Irene Hunt	Follett	1967
The King's Fifth	Scott O'Dell	Houghton Mifflin	1967
Zlateh the Goat and Other Stories	Isaac Bashevis singer	Harper	1967
The Jazz Man	Mary H, Weik	Atheneum	1967
I, Juan de Pareja	Elizabeth Borton de Trevino	Farrar	1966

NEWBERY AWARD WINNERS

Book Title	Author	Publisher	Year Published
The Black Cauldron	Lloyd Alexander	Holt	1966
The Animal Family	Randall Jarrell	Pantheon	1966
The Noonday Friends	Mary Stolz	Harper	1966
Shadow of a Bull	Maia Wojciechowska	Atheneum	1965
Across Five Aprils	Irene Hunt	Follett	1965
It's Like This, Cat	Emily Neville	Harper	1964
Rascal: A Memoir of a Better Era	Sterling North	Dutton	1964
The Loner	Esther Wier	McKay/Longman	1964
A Wrinkle in Time	Madeleine L'Engle	Farrar	1963
Thistle and Thyme: Tales and Legends from Scotland	Sorche Nic Leodhas	Holt	1963
Men of Athens	Olivia Coolidge	Houghton Mifflin	1963
The Bronze Bow	Elizabeth George Speare	Houghton Mifflin	1962
Frontier Living	Edwin Tunis	World	1962
The Golden Goblet	Eloise J. McGraw	Coward	1962
Belling the Tiger	Mary Stolz	Harper	1962
Island of the Blue Dolphins	Scott O'Dell	Houghton Mifflin	1961
America Moves Forward	Gerald Johnson	Morrow	1961
Old Ramon	Jack Schaefer	Houghton Mifflin	1961
The Cricket in Times Square	George Selden	Farrar	1961
Onion John	Joseph Krumgold	Crowell	1960
My Side of the Mountain	Jean Craighead George	Dutton	1960
America Is Born	Gerald Johnson	Morrow	1960
The Gammage Cup	Carol Kendall	Harcourt	1960
The Witch of Blackbird Pond	Elizabeth George Speare	Houghton Mifflin	1959
The Family under the Bridge	Natalie S. Carlson	Harper	1959
Along Came a Dog	Meindert DeJong	Harper	1959
Chucaro: Wild Pony of the Pampa	Francis Kalnay	Harcourt	1959
The Perilous Road	William O. Steele	Harcourt	1959
Rifles for Watie	Harold Keith	Crowell	1958
The Horsecatcher	Mari Sondoz	Westminster	1958
Gone-Away Lake	Elizaabeth Enright	Harcourt	1958
The Great Wheel	Robert Lawson	Viking	1958
Tom Paine, Freedom's Apostle	Leo Gurko	Crowell	1958
Miracles on Maple Hill	Virginia Sorenson	Harcourt	1957
Old Yeller	Fred Gipson	Harper	1957

NEWBERY AWARD WINNERS

Book Title	Author	Publisher	Year Published
The House of Sixty Fathers	Meindert DeJong	Harper	1957
Mr. Justice Holmes	Clara I. Judson	Follett	1957
The Corn Grows Ripe	Dorothy Rhoads	Viking	1957
The Black Fox of Lorne	Marguerite de Angeli	Doubleday	1957
Carry On, Mr. Bowditch	Jean Lee Latham	Houghton Mifflin	1956
The Golden Name Day	Jennie D. Lindquist	Harper	1956
The Secret River	Marjorie Kinnan Rawlings	Scribner's	1956
Men, Microscopes and Living Things	Kaatherine B. Shippen	Viking	1956
The Wheel on the School	Meindert DeJong	Harper	1955
The Courage of Sarah Noble	Alice Dalgliesch	Scribner's	1955
Banner in the Sky	James Ramsey Ullman	Lippincott	1955
. . . And Now Miguel	Joseph Krumgold	Crowell	1954
Secret of the Andes	Ann Nolan Clark	Viking	1953
Ginger Pye	Eleanor Estes	Harcourt	1952
Amos Fortune, Free Man	Elizabeth Yates	Dutton	1951
The Door in the Wall	Marguerite de Angeli	Doubleday	1950
King of the Wind	Marguerite Henry	Rand McNally	1949
The Twenty-One Baloons	William Pene du Bois	Viking	1948
Miss Hickory	Carolyn Sherwin Bailey	Viking	1947
Strawberry Girl	Lois Lenski	Lippincott	1946
Rabbit Hill	Robert Lawson	Viking	1945
Johnny Tremain	Esther Forbes	Houghton Mifflin	1944
Adam of the Road	Elizabeth Jane Gray	Viking	1943
The Matchlock Gun	Walter Edmonds	Dodd	1942
Call It Courage	Armstrong Sperry	Macmillan	1941
Daniel Boone	James Daugherty	Viking	1940
Thimble Summer	Elizabeth Enright	Rinehart	1939
The White Stag	Kate Seredy	Viking	1938
Roller Skates	Ruth Sawyer	Viking	1937
Caddie Woodlawn	Carol Ryrie Brink	Macmillan	1936
Dobry	Monica Shannon	Viking	1935
Invincible Louisa: The Story of the Author of Little Women	Cornelia Meigs	Little, Brown	1934
Young Fu of the Upper Yangtze	Elizabeth Lewis	Winston	1933
Waterless Mountain	Larua Adams Armer	Longmans	1932

NEWBERY AWARD WINNERS

Book Title	Author	Publisher	Year Published
The Cat Who Went to Heaven	Elizabeth Coatsworth	Macmillan	1931
Hitty, Her First Hundred Years	Rachel Field	Macmillan	1930
The Trumpeter of Krakow	Eric P. Kelly	Macmillan	1929
Gay Neck, the Story of a Pigeon	Dhan Gopal Mukerji	Dutton	1928
Smoky, the Cowhorse	Will James	Scribner	1927
Shen of the Sea	Arthur Bowie Chrisman	Dutton	1926
Tales from Silver Lands	Charles Finger	Doubleday	1925
The Dark Frigate	Charles Hawes	Little, Brown	1924
The Voyages of Doctor Dolittle	Hugh Lofting	Lippincott	1923
The Story of Mankind	Hendrik Willem van Loon	Liveright	1922

GLOSSARY

I. Standards for Comprehension

Activate and Apply Prior Knowledge. Prior knowledge is what someone already knows. Strategic readers bring their prior knowledge to a text. Using prior knowledge helps readers understand characters and events in fiction and can help a reader better negotiate a nonfiction text in determining what he or she already knows and what further information may be found in the text. Learners continually add new information to their schema, turning new knowledge into prior knowledge!

Analyze Critically. Students should be able to offer an opinion about the selection, a character, the craft, or other element of literary structure. Opinions should be supported with a justification from life experience, comparison to another selection, emotional response, or direct evidence from the text.

Compare/Contrast. If you compare two things, you tell how they are alike. If you contrast them, you tell how they are different. As readers encounter different texts, they may compare characters, setting, text structures, and/or plots of texts.

Construct Sensory Images. Sensory images engage a reader's senses of taste, touch, sight, smell, or hearing. Strategic readers pause to visualize what the author is describing so that all the details come alive in their minds. When students write, they should focus on creating images that engage their readers' senses.

Determine Importance. Strategic readers determine which information in a text is important to understanding the ideas the author presents. While some details are important, others are details that may just be "interesting." Text structure often helps readers determine which information is important. Readers might look for special fonts, cue words, and text organizers. Illustrations and photographs often cue what information is important to understanding a text.

Determine Purpose. An author's purpose is the author's reason for writing a piece of text. Authors write for three main purposes: to inform or teach readers about something, to entertain readers, or to persuade or convince the audience to do or not do something. Readers read for a variety of purposes, including to be entertained, to be informed, to enjoy the art in a piece of text, to savor the language, and so on. As students become more strategic readers, they understand that they read differently depending on the purpose of the reading.

Draw and Support Conclusions. Good readers "read between the lines." Often, they draw conclusions, determining ideas that are not directly stated in the text. A reader draws a conclusion by considering clues in the text and what he or she already knows about something. Good readers and writers can support their conclusions with relevant references to the text.

Form Literal and Interpretive Questions. As students read, they should stop to ask questions of their own. As they generate questions, they become aware of whether they can answer their questions and whether they understand what they are reading. Literal questions help readers restate what is in the text. Interpretive questions help them think beyond the author's words, leading them to deeper thought and eventually deeper understanding of what they have read.

Identify Cause and Effect. An effect is something that happens, while a cause is an event that leads to that effect. Getting wet, for example, is an effect caused by getting caught in a rainstorm without an umbrella. Writers can use cause and effect to organize a text. Some words, such as *because* and *as a result*, signify causes and effects. To determine cause and effect, readers should ask "What happened? Why did it happen?"

Infer. When readers infer, they create personal meaning from a text. Inferring involves a mental process of combining what is read with prior knowledge, or schema. Blending elements of text and schema leads to a reader's unique interpretation. As readers infer, they can predict and revise their predictions, use their background knowledge along with information in the text to answer questions they have as they read, make connections, and make critical judgments about what they read.

Interpret. An interpretation is an expression of understanding in your own words. Students may use stems such as, "I think that means..." "The big idea is ..." "It didn't say this in the book, but I think we should notice that..." These interpretations support critical analysis, connections and deeper level understanding.

Identify Main Ideas. The main idea is the focus of a text or section of text, the most important idea. Supporting details are bits of information that tell more about the main idea. Strategic readers learn to distinguish important information from bits of supporting information. They use details to support their identification of a main idea.

Make Connections. Strategic readers use their background knowledge, or schema, to enhance their understanding of the text. Readers connect to text in several ways. They can use information from their own lives and apply that information to what they read in a text. Readers can also make connections to other selections they have read or to their knowledge of the world.

Represent Text with an Organizer. When learners can represent understanding through a chart, a graph, a story map or a sketch, they must move information from one communication system into another. For example, they heard the story through their auditory system, now they must use a visual system to represent understanding as they use a Venn diagram to compare lead characters. Graphic representations are well supported by brain research and are helpful tools for all learners.

Summarize. When readers summarize, they choose the most important facts that make up the main idea of a passage. Summarization means picking out the facts that are important and that make up the main idea of the passage. A reader demonstrates understanding of the text

when he or she can choose the most important details and put them in his or her own words in a summary.

II. Standards for Structural Elements

Character. A character is any person or animal who takes part in the action of a story.

Character Development. An author can develop a character in several ways. An author might simply describe a character, telling readers what the character looks like. An author can develop a character by showing what the character says, does, and thinks. The character's actions, thoughts, and words reveal what that character is like. Finally, an author can show what a character is like by highlighting the reactions and opinions of other characters.

Climax. The climax is the turning point of the action in the plot of a story or a play. This "high point" of the story usually indicates the outcome of a story.

Conclusion. The conclusion is where everything comes together and you get a clear sense that the plot is ending. In the conclusion, you often see that a problem has been solved. The conclusion is not necessarily the last event in a selection. See **Falling Action.**

Dialogue. The dialogue in a selection is the words that are spoken by the characters. Dialogue is set apart by quotation marks.

Falling Action. The events that happen after the climax in a story are the falling action. This is when the author finishes the story and gives it a closing.

Illustration. Pictures are an essential support system in picture books. They often expand and elaborate upon the meaning conveyed in the text. Teaching our students to pay attention to illustrations and to notice mood, tone, and details will enhance their understanding, help them make stronger connections, and help them develop a rich appreciation for the gorgeous art that is so often present in these mentor selections.

Initiating Event. This is the event in which the problem of the selection becomes apparent, not necessarily the first event in the selection.

Main Idea. The main idea of a text is its central thought or message. While the topic of a text is the subject of that text, the main idea is the thought that is being expressed about the topic. The main idea is what the author wants readers to remember, that is, his or her general point about a topic. A main idea is often stated or suggested early in a text.

Mood. Mood is the overall atmosphere of the story.

Plot. The plot is the series of related events that make up a story. A plot can be focused on a conflict between two characters, between a character and some external force, or between a character and him- or herself (an inner conflict). A plot may follow a sequence of time order, may be circular (once a resolution happens, the plot begins again), or may be focused on a problem that is solved in the end.

Problem/Solution Structure. A story is usually set in motion when characters are presented with a problem or problems that they must solve. Events occur as they look for solutions to those problems. Strategic readers can identify the events that are most important to the structure of the story. In nonfiction they can identify the steps that lead to the solution to a problem.

Setting. The setting is the time and place in which a story occurs. The setting provides a backdrop for a story, but it also can add atmosphere and mood to a text. The setting can also affect the characters and maybe even the events in a story.

Theme. The theme of a piece of fiction answers the question, "What is this text all about?" The theme is an overall message of a piece. The theme provides unity in the piece by following one central idea throughout the story.

Tone. Tone is the author's attitude about characters and situations, revealed in word choice and details. Tone includes an author's moral view of a situation.

III. Standards for Vocabulary/ Literary Language

Alliteration Alliteration is the repetition of a consonant sound at the beginning of words, as in "Seven silver swans swam silently seaward." Alliteration emphasizes certain words by making them stand out.

Context Clues. Context clues are hints in a text that lead a reader to figure out the meanings of words he or she does not know. The clues might be before, within, or after a sentence containing an unknown word. Specific kinds of context clues include definitions, synonyms, antonyms, or examples.

Literary Language. Literary language includes story language such as "once upon a time." It is more formal than daily speech, yet it may feel familiar because many stories use common elements of literary language.

Figurative Language. This is language that evokes sensory images or makes comparisons. Figurative language assists the reader by creating strong images, and it can be used in fiction and nonfiction.

Metaphor. A metaphor is a figure of speech that compares two unlike things that have some element in common. A metaphor makes a comparison without using the words *like* or *as*.

Multiple-Meaning Words A multiple-meaning word has more than one meaning. To understand the meaning, we have to think about the other words in the sentence, or the context. See **Context Clues.**

Onomatopoeia. Onomatopoeia is the use of words to imitate sounds. Some examples are *shush, hiss, whack,* and *zoom.*

Repetition. Repetition is the duplication of a sound, a word, or a group of words. Writers use repetition to emphasize whatever it is that is repeated. Something that is repeated stands out, helping the reader know that idea, sound, or word is important.

Simile. A simile is a comparison between two unlike things that have something in common.

Unlike a metaphor, a simile always uses the words *like* or *as* to make a comparison.

Transition Words. Transition words such as *before, after, now, first, then, finally, next, after, but, soon, once, now, right before, whenever,* and *one day* help readers make logical connections between sentences, paragraphs, and ideas in a text. Transitional words function as signs for readers that tell them how to think about, organize, and react to ideas as they read through text.

Word Meanings. Readers need an array of strategies for determining the meaning of words. Strategies include using context clues, root words, word parts such as prefixes and suffixes, and what they know about multiple-meaning words. Sometimes a dictionary can help. (Also see **Context Clues** and **Multiple-Meaning Words**.)

IV. Standards for Literary Elements and Devices

Allusion. In a text, an allusion is a reference to a famous person, place, thing or part of another text. For the allusion to be effective, the reader needs to know the text that is being alluded to.

Hyperbole/Obvious Exaggeration. Hyperbole is an exaggeration so obvious that it can't be missed, such as "I was so shocked, you could have knocked me over with a feather." A writer often uses hyperbole to make a point by overstating it or to add humor to a piece of writing.

Flashback. A flashback is a scene in a story that returns to an earlier time, telling what happened before. An author uses flashbacks to "fill in" the story for readers. A writer might also use flashback to emphasize an event in the story by comparing it to something that happened before.

Foreshadowing. Foreshadowing is the use of clues or hints to suggest what will happen later in a story. Foreshadowing can build suspense in a story. Foreshadowing can also make a story more believable—the reader is prepared for events that will come later in the story.

Imagery. Imagery is created when an author weaves words together to create mental images that activate the reader's senses. Imagery assists the reader to visualize or feel what the author is describing.

Irony. When there is a contrast between what we expect and what happens, then we have irony. Here is an example: If it is raining really hard, we would expect someone to say "Wow. It is miserable outside today." If instead I say "Nice day," that is irony.

Personification. Personification is giving human qualities, feelings, action, or characteristics to inanimate (non-living) objects. *The wind sang a mournful song* and *The water invited swimmers to jump in* are both examples of personification. The wind and water are given the human abilities to sing and invite.

Poetic Justice. Poetic justice is a tool authors use in which bad is punished and good is rewarded. In poetic justice, the "punishment" for the bad is usually really a good match to what the individual did wrong. It is important that any "punishment" does not cause lasting harm.

Point of View. A story is told from a certain vantage point. That vantage point is the point of view. In the first-person point of view, the narrator is a participant in the story. Stories told from the first person point of view have the word *I*. In the third-person point of view, the narrator is someone outside the story.

Symbolism. A symbol is an object or an action that has additional meaning beyond itself. Authors use symbolism to represent important ideas.

V. Standards for Genre

Biography. This is a nonfiction genre that outlines the life or a portion of the life of a real person in history.

Fairy Tale. A fairy tale is a very old story with magical events often passed along by word of mouth. Fairy tales contain such elements as magical characters, royalty, giants, witches, and talking animals. Settings for fairy tales include castles, cottages, mountains, rivers, forests, and gardens. Fairy tales often have similar plots, such as a hero fighting a villain, a transformation, a hero rewarded with wealth, and so on.

Fantasy. In the genre of fantasy, we expect imaginary worlds and magical or supernatural events. This is fiction that is carried beyond the realm of what might happen in the real world.

Fiction. Fiction texts are storytelling, or imagined events. Types of fiction include novels, short stories, fables, tall tales, fairy tales, historical fiction, and realistic fiction. Fiction may be partly based on factual events, but all fiction contains some elements that come from the imaginations of writers. Many readers think of fiction as literature that is written as art or to entertain readers. Fiction often evokes strong emotions in its readers.

Folktale. A folk tale is a story or legend handed down from generation to generation usually by oral retelling. Folk tales often explain something that happens in nature or convey a certain truth about life.

Historical Fiction. Historical fiction is a story created by the author but designed to reflect the way life really was at a certain time in history. The setting and details are rooted in historical fact.

Nonfiction. Nonfiction is writing based on fact instead of on imaginary events. Nonfiction deals with real people, events, and experiences. There are many types of nonfiction, including autobiographies, biographies, and essays.

Poetry. In the genre of poetry, writers use imagery and precise word choices to convey their feelings about a topic. Poetry is often written in lines and verses. Not all poems rhyme.

Tall Tale. A tall tale is a type of folktale that includes hyperbole and larger-than-life characters.

VI. Standards for Writing Traits

Conventions. Conventions are a support system writers offer to their readers. Conventional spacing, spelling, grammar, punctuation, and capitalization help a reader use what he or she knows about the act of reading to navigate a piece of writing. It is about consistency and politeness. But, it is also developmental; that is, readers master conventions gradually as they gain experience with a variety of texts. The message is the central focus, with support from conventions.

Ideas Ideas are the core of any piece of writing. They are the focus that marries a main idea with the details that bring life to a piece of writing. Writing that has strong ideas at the core is interesting to the reader and joyful for the writer to create. Ideas and content are developed when rich details illuminate both the illustrations and the written text.

Organization Writing needs to have a structure that holds it together. There must be a skeleton that everything else is built around. Organization can be reflected in the way illustrations and text are laid out on the page, in the sequence of events, or by a clear beginning and ending to a piece of writing.

Sentence Fluency Oral language has natural rhythm and flow. There is a sense of connection between the sentences and a rich variety in sentence length. When writers have sentence fluency, reading their work aloud is highly satisfying as the sentences flow one into another.

Voice Voice is the writer coming to life through the words on the page. It is the uniqueness of the individual behind the pen becoming apparent to the reader. It can be a glimmer of humor, a bit of creativity, or a feeling of enthusiasm that gives the reader a window into the presence of the author.

Word Choice Precise, colorful word choices bring clarity to writing and add interest for the reader. When young writers stretch their "vocabulary muscles" to use words that are new, words that are unusual, or old words in new combinations, they are helping their reader understand more deeply.

GRAPHIC ORGANIZERS

STORY MAP

Title: _____

Author: _____

Climax:

Major Characters:
Minor Characters:

8. _____

7. _____

6. _____

5. _____

4. _____

3. _____

2. _____

Initiating Event

1. _____

Introduction

Rising Action/Events

Falling Action/Conclusion

9. _____

10. _____

Conflict:

Resolution:

Setting:

Author's Theme:

PROBLEM/SOLUTION STORY CHART

Title: _____ Author:_____

Setting: Characters:

The Problem:

Events/Steps Toward Solving the Problem:

-
-
-
-
-
-

Solution:

IDENTIFYING PURPOSES CHART

Title	Kind of Text	Author's Purpose	Reader's Purpose	Reader's Approach

CHARACTER ORGANIZER

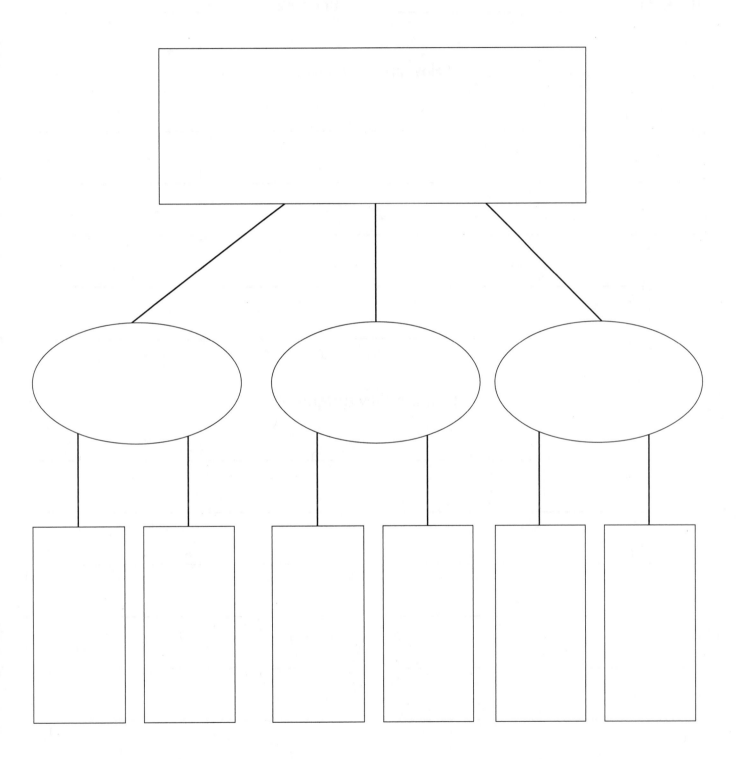

COMPARE/CONTRAST CHART

Book #1 _____   Book #2 _____

How are they alike?

_____

_____

_____

_____

How are they different?

_____	_____
_____	_____
_____	_____
_____	_____
_____	_____

PLOT ORGANIZER

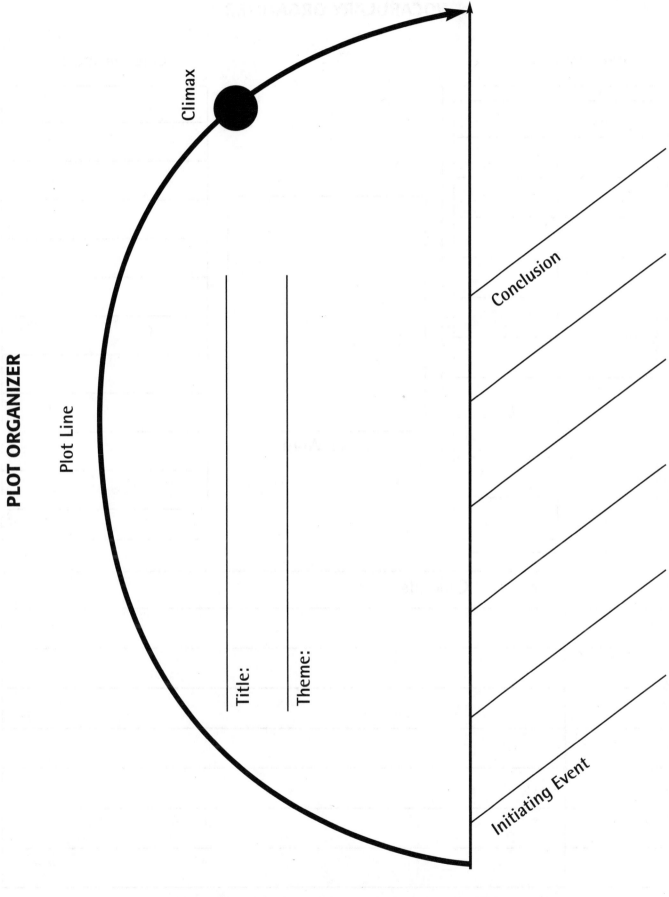

Plot Line

Climax

Conclusion

Title:

Theme:

Initiating Event

VOCABULARY ORGANIZER

Word Predictions

word	✓

Core Vocabulary

Focus Word

	Important Concepts
1.	

ALPHABOX

The Book: _____

The Reader (s) _____

A	B	C	D
E	F	G	H
I	J	K	L
M	N	O	P
Q	R	S	T
U	V	W	XYZ

VOICE CHECKLIST

_____ The author shows passion for the topic.

_____ The author's opinions are understood through the writing.

_____ The author captured a tone or mood with words.

_____ If humor is used, it is appropriate for the topic and format.

ELEMENTS OF SENTENCE FLUENCY CHART

Elements of Sentence Fluency	Book _____ _____ ✓ if element is present	Book _____ _____ ✓ if element is present	Book _____ _____ ✓ if element is present	Book _____ _____ ✓ if element is present
Sentences vary in length.				
Sentences flow together.				
The piece appeals to the ear when read aloud.				

SENTENCE FLUENCY CHECKLIST

_____ Sentences mostly begin with different words.

_____ There is a mixture of simple and complex sentences.

_____ Transitional words link sentences.

_____ When read aloud, there is a rhythm in the sentences.

BIBLIOGRAPHY OF PROFESSIONAL RESOURCES

Britton, J. 1970. *Language and Learning*. Harmondsworth, Middlesex, UK: Penguin.

Cary, Stephen. 2000. *Working with Second Language Learners: Answers to Teachers' Top Ten Questions*. Portsmouth, NH: Heinemann.

Cullinan, B. and D. Person. 2005. *Continuum Encyclopedia of Children's Literature*. London: Continuum International Publishing Group.

Culham, R. and Vicki Spandel. 1996. *Picture Books: An Annotated Bibliography for Teaching Writing*. Portland, Oregon: NW Regional Educational Laboratory.

Fountas, Irene C. and Gay Su Pinnell. 2006. *Teaching for Comprehending and Fluency: Thinking, Talking, and Writing About Reading, K–8*. Portsmouth, NH: Heinemann.

Hall, Susan. 1994. *Using Picture Storybooks to Teach Literary Devices*. Phoenix, AZ: Oryz Press.

Holdaway, Don. 1979. *Foundations of Literacy*. Portsmouth, NH: Heinemann.

Hoyt, L. and Teresa Therriault. 2007. *Mastering the Mechanics: Lessons for Modeled, Guided, and Independent Writing; grades 4/5*. New York, NY: Scholastic.

Hoyt, Linda 1999. *Revisit, Reflect, Retell*. Portsmouth, NH: Heinemann.
    2000. *Snapshots: Literacy Minilessons Up Close*. Portsmouth, NH: Heinemann.
    2001. *Snapshots: The Video*. Portsmouth, NH: Heinemann.
    2003. *Make It Real*. Portsmouth, NH: Heinemann.
    2004. *Navigating Informational Texts*. Portsmouth, NH: Heinemann.
    2005. *Spotlight on Comprehension*. Portsmouth, NH: Heinemann.

Hoyt, Linda, Margaret Mooney, and Brenda Parkes. 2004. *Exploring Informational Texts*. Portsmouth, NH: Heinemann.

Huck, C. and B. Zulandt Kiefer. 2004. *Children's Literature in the Elementary School*. New York: McGraw Hill.

Jensen, E. 1998. *Teaching with the Brain in Mind*. Alexandria, VA: ASCD.

Laminack, Lester, and Reba M. Wadsworth. 2006. *Learning Under the Influence of Language and Literature: Making the Most of Read-Alouds Across the Day*. Portsmouth, NH: Heinemann.

McMahon, Carolyn and Peggy Warrick. *Wee Can Write*. 2005. Portland, OR: Northwest Regional Educational Laboratory.

National Center on Education and the Economy. 2001. *Performance Standards, Volume 1*. Pittsburgh, PA: Harcourt.

Parkes, Brenda. 2003. *Read It Again*. York, ME: Stenhouse.

Pearson, P. David and M. C. Gallagher. 1983. "The Instruction of Reading Comprehension." *Contemporary Educational Psychology* 8, pp. 317–344.

Rasinski, T. 2004. *The Fluent Reader*. New York: Scholastic.

Routman, Regie. 2003. *Reading Essentials: The Specifics You Need to Teach Reading Well.* Portsmouth, NH: Heinemann.

Wolfe, Patricia. 2001. *Brain Matters: Translating Research into Classroom Practice.* Alexandria, VA: ASCD.